VOCA … Y

for the College Bound

BOOK A

2nd Edition

Revised and Expanded

ISBN 978-1-62019-111-8

Senior Editor: Paul Moliken

Editor: Darlene Gilmore

Cover & Text Design: Larry Knox

Layout: Chris Koniencki

P.O. Box 658 Clayton, Delaware 19938 • www.prestwickhouse.com

Item No. 309268

Table *of* Contents

Strategies for Completing Activities

Lessons

Strategies *for* Completing Activities

Words in Context

One way you can make sure that you understand what an unfamiliar word means is to see it used in a sentence and make a guess, an inference, as to its meaning. For example, you probably do not know what the word *theriomorphic* means. Using roots, prefixes, and suffixes will help, as you will see explained below. Read it in the following sentence, though, and you will have another method to arrive at its meaning:

> The drawing on the clay tablet that archaeologists recently discovered depicted a man with antlers and hooves—a *theriomorphic* being—within a ring of fire.

Clues in the sentence enable you to see the context of *theriomorphic*: a primitive drawing showing something not completely human. Therefore, you can infer that *theriomorphic* means "a person who looks like an animal."

Here's another example:

> Dawn was a *somnambulist*; on some nights, her family found her in the hall, other times she was discovered in the basement, and once, they found her sitting asleep in the front seat of the car.

After reading the sentence, you should be able to infer that the word *somnambulist* must mean someone who walks in his or her sleep.

Roots, Prefixes, and Suffixes

To the person interested in words, a knowledge of roots, prefixes, and suffixes turns each new, unfamiliar word into a puzzle. And while it is a sure and lifelong way to build your vocabulary, there are two points to keep in mind.

1. Some words have evolved through usage so that today's definitions are different from the ones you might have inferred from an examination of their roots and/or prefixes. For example, the word *abstruse* contains the prefix *ab–* (away) and the root *trudere* (to thrust) and literally means "to thrust away." But today, the word is used to describe something that is "hard to understand."

2. Occasionally, you may go wrong on a root. For example, knowing that the root *vin* means "to conquer," you would be correct in concluding that the word *invincible* means "not able to be conquered"; but if you tried to apply that root meaning to the word *vindictive* or *vindicate*, you would miss the mark. So, in analyzing an unfamiliar word, check for other possible roots than the one you first assumed if your inferred meaning doesn't fit the context.

These warnings notwithstanding, a knowledge of roots, prefixes, and suffixes is one of the best ways to build a strong, vital vocabulary.

Usage Inferences

The next method of determining if you understand what a word means is for you to see the word as it might be applied to various situations. Therefore, in a Usage Inference, you need to be able to take the definition you learned into the real world. Remembering the definition and using the word correctly are two different concepts. We supply a series of multiple-choice situations in which you need to figure out the best use of the word.

Let's assume that you learned in a lesson that *specious* means "false or faulty reasoning that seems true" or "an argument that does not stand up to logical reasoning."

Example:

When or where would making a *specious* argument most likely be challenged?
A. on Friday night asking for the keys to the family car
B. in a jury room debating the guilt of someone on trial
C. with your family deciding on the price of a trip to Hawaii
D. at school trying to convince your friend to go sky diving

While all the answers could be examples of making a specious argument, the one that might cause a problem is B, simply because any faulty argument would most likely be argued against by another juror. Obviously, faulty logic and arguments can be used in A, B, C, and D. After all, saying the wrong thing may prevent getting the keys, spending too much could ruin a trip, and sky diving is dangerous. These three situations, though, are less likely to have flawed logic called into question.

Another key to the correct answer is stated in the question, so make sure that you read that part carefully, as it frequently will narrow down your choices.

Reading Comprehension

Reading questions generally fall into several types.

1. *Identifying the main idea or the author's purpose. In short, the question asks, "What is this selection about?"*

   In some paragraphs, this is easy to spot because there are one or two ideas that leap from the paragraph. In some selections, however, this may be much more difficult, especially if there are convoluted sentences with clauses embedded within clauses. It also may be difficult in those selections in which there are inverted sentences (a sentence with the subject at the end) or elliptical sentences (a sentence in which a word or words are left out). All of these obstacles, however, can be overcome if you take one sentence at a time and put it in your own words.

Consider the following sentence:

These writers either jot down their thoughts bit by bit, in short, ambiguous, and paradoxical sentences, which apparently mean much more than they say—of this kind of writing Schelling's treatises on natural philosophy are a splendid instance; or else they hold forth with a deluge of words and the most intolerable diffusiveness, as though no end of fuss were necessary to make the reader understand the deep meaning of their sentences, whereas it is some quite simple if not actually trivial idea, examples of which may be found in plenty in the popular works of Fichte, and the philosophical manuals of a hundred other miserable dunces.

But if we edit out some of the words, the main point of this sentence is obvious.

These writers either jot down their thoughts bit by bit, in short, ambiguous, and paradoxical sentences, which apparently mean much more than they say—of this kind of writing Schelling's treatises on natural philosophy are a splendid instance; or else they hold forth with a deluge of words and the most intolerable diffusiveness, as though [it] end of fuss were necessary to make the reader understand the deep meaning of their sentences, whereas it is som [a]uite simple if not actually trivial idea, examples of which may be found in plenty in the popular works of Fichte, and the philosophical manuals of a hundred other miserable dunces.

While the previous sentence needs only deletions to make it clear, this next one requires major revisions and must be read carefully and put into the reader's own words.

Some in their discourse desire rather commendation of wit, in being able to hold all arguments, than of judgment, in discerning what is true; as if it were a praise to know what might be said, and not what should be thought.

After studying it, a reader might revise the sentence as follows:

In their conversations, some people would rather win praise for their wit or style of saying something rather than win praise for their ability to judge between what is true or false—as if it were better to sound good regardless of the quality of thought.

2. *Identifying the stated or inferred meaning.* Simply, what is the author stating or suggesting?

3. *Identifying the tone or mood of the selection or the author's feeling.*

To answer this type of question, look closely at individual words and their connotations. For example, if an author describes one person as stubborn and another as firm, it tells you something of the author's feelings. In the same manner, if the author uses many words with harsh, negative connotations, he is conveying one mood; but if he uses words with milder negative connotations, he may be striving for quite another mood.

Pronunciation Guide

ă ....pat
ā ....aid, fey, pay
â ....air, care, wear, ant
ä ....father
b ....bib
ch ....church
d ....deed
ĕ ....pet, pleasure
ē ....be, bee, easy, leisure
f ....fast, fife, off, phase, rough
g ....gag
h ....hat
hw ......which
ĭ ....pit
ī ....by, guy, pie
î ....dear, deer, fierce, mere
j ....jury, joke
k ....kiss, clean, quit
oi ....soil, toy
ou ....cow, out
ŏ ....closet, bother
ō ....boat, oh
ŏŏ ....took
ōō ....boot, fruit
ô ....ball, haul
p ....pop
r ....roar
s ....miss, sauce, see
sh ....dish, ship
t ....tight
th ....path, thin
th ....this, bathe
ŭ ....cut, rough
û ....circle, firm, heard, term, turn, urge, word
v ....cave, valve, vine
w ....with
y ....yes
yōō .....abuse, use
z ....rose, size, xylophone, zebra
zh ....garage, pleasure, vision
ə ....about, silent, pencil, lemon, circus
ər ....butter

Lesson One

1. **adjunct** (adj´ ungkt) *noun* a subordinate; an assistant
adj. added or connected in a dependent or subordinate manner
Before his dismissal, Dr. Jones had been an *adjunct* professor at the university.
syn: addition, appendage, attachment

2. **admonish** (ăd mŏn´ ĭsh) *verb* to warn, to caution
The lifeguard *admonished* the small children about the high waves and undertow before allowing them to go near the water.
syn: advise, notify

3. **advocate** (ăd´ və kāt) *verb* to recommend; to speak in favor of
I would *advocate* a telephone survey to find out if there is backing for the proposed changes.
syn: prescribe, support *ant:* oppose, contest

4. **affiliate** (ə fil´ ē ĭt) *noun* an associate, partner
He denied that he was an *affiliate* of any organized-crime figure.
syn: member, subordinate, employee

5. **affliction** (ə flĭk´ shən) *noun* anything causing great suffering
His nightly insomnia is an *affliction* that has caused many problems at work.
syn: trouble, pain, distress *ant:* relief, aid

6. **aghast** (ə găst´) *adj.* feeling great dismay or horror
We were *aghast* at the sarcastic tone the teenage girl directed at her parents.
syn: terrified, shocked, amazed

7. **alacrity** (ə lăk´ rĭ tē) *noun* liveliness; willingness; eagerness
He performed his chores with *alacrity*.
syn: promptness, briskness, readiness *ant:* slowness, reluctance

8. **alienate** (āl´ yə nāt) *verb* to make others unfriendly toward you
Don't *alienate* your neighbors unless you really like to be alone.
syn: estrange, turn against

9. **allude** (ə lōōd´) *verb* to hint at; to refer to indirectly
The attorney *alluded* to a cover-up but was not very specific.
syn: suggest, refer, imply

10. **aloof** (ə lōōf´) *adj.* reserved, distant
The singer looked rather *aloof* as he stood on the step signing autographs in a bored manner.
syn: remote, cool, indifferent *ant:* warm, friendly

Exercise I Words in Context

Fill in the blanks with the correct vocabulary words needed to complete the sentences.

affliction **adjunct** **alluded** **advocate** **aghast**

A. When his ________________ assistant got a promotion, the professor advertised in the local newspaper for a new one. When the first applicant arrived for his interview, Dr. Smith was ________________ at his inappropriate appearance. He looked like he was suffering from the ________________ of homelessness.

B. Although the speaker ________________ to taking drastic action, he was careful not to ________________ violence as the solution.

affiliated **alienated** **aloof** **admonished** **alacrity**

C. While some of the guests remained ________________, others joined in the activity with ________________.

D. Although his wife had ________________ Mr. Jones about his behavior, he ________________ just about everyone in the neighborhood, and now, no one speaks to him. He claims that he prefers not being ________________ with anyone or anything in the neighborhood.

Exercise II Roots, Prefixes, and Suffixes

Study the entries and answer the questions that follow.

The prefix *sub–* means "under, below." The suffix *–ize* means "to make."
The root *urb* means "city."

1. Without using a dictionary, try to define the following words:
   suburb standardize
   urbanize subhuman
   substandard humanize

2. The action of many people leaving cities and moving into the ________________ causes the cities to decay. This results in what is called ________________ blight.

3. List as many words as you can think of that use the prefix *sub–*, the suffix *–ize*, or the root *urb*.

Exercise III Usage Inferences

Choose the answer that best fits the situation.

1. Who is least likely to move with *alacrity*?
   A. someone walking for exercise
   B. a person going to a job interview
   C. a teenager doing chores
   D. someone trying to meet a deadline

2. If you are *aloof*, in which job would you most likely not do well?
   A. policeman
   B. plumber
   C. teacher
   D. salesman

3. Who would most likely *advocate* the releasing of wolves into remote national parks?
   A. a conservationist
   B. a veterinarian
   C. a rancher
   D. a supermarket executive

Exercise IV Reading Comprehension

Read the selection and answer the questions.

Some books are to be tasted, others to be swallowed, and some few to be chewed and digested; that is, some books are to be read only in parts; others to be read, but not curiously; and some few wholly, and with diligence and attention. Some books also may be read by deputy, and extracts made of them by others; but that would be only in the less important arguments, and the meaner sort of books; else distilled books are like common distilled waters, flashy things.

Francis Bacon

1. The author's main point in this selection is that
   A. it is quite acceptable to read extracts of books.
   B. all books should be read in the same fashion.
   C. not all books should be read in the same way.
   D. books are no substitute for experience.

2. The tone of this selection is one of
   A. repressed anger.
   B. hopeless sadness.
   C. biting satire.
   D. thoughtful reflection.

3. Of "distilled books" the author thinks
   A. they are trash that no one should read.
   B. they have a great deal of importance to say.
   C. they may be read by others and reported on.
   D. they are to be chewed and digested.

4. The author implies or states that
   A. all books are worth our full attention.
   B. some books should be read only very quickly or in part.
   C. mean books are not worth reading because of the violence in them.
   D. every book an author feels is important enough to be written is important enough to be read.

Lesson Two

1. **amalgamate** (ə măl´ gə māt) *verb* to combine
Because of his forceful personality, he was able to *amalgamate* the smaller tribes into a large and dangerous army.
syn: unite, blend, mix, consolidate *ant*: splinter, disunite

2. **ambidextrous** (ăm bĭ dĕk´ strəs) *adj.* equally skillful with either hand
Because he was *ambidextrous*, he was good at pitching horseshoes with either hand.
syn: versatile

3. **anachronism** (ă năk´ rə nĭz əm) *noun* something or someone out of its proper time
The setting for the play was a peasant village in the Middle Ages, but in the middle of the stage was a refrigerator. What an *anachronism* that was!

4. **animate** (ăn´ ə māt) *verb* to give life or motion to
Even a trip to the ice cream parlor did little to *animate* the two tired children.
syn: enliven, encourage, excite *ant*: deaden

5. **anthropomorphic** (ăn thrə pə môr´ fĭk) *adj.* attributing human characteristics or qualities to objects, animals, or gods
I just hate *anthropomorphic* stories in which pigs and rabbits walk upright, dress in clothes, and speak to each other in a human tongue.

6. **antiquated** (ăn´ tĭ kwā tĭd) *adj.* no longer used or useful; very old
The *antiquated* car chugged slowly up the hill.
syn: obsolete, outdated *ant*: current, new

7. **aphorism** (ăf´ ə rĭz əm) *noun* a concise statement of a truth or principle
"Waste not, want not" is an *aphorism* that my father lives by.
syn: proverb, adage, maxim

8. **aplomb** (ə plăm´) *noun* self-confidence
The youngest dancer showed such *aplomb* that even the veterans of the troupe were astonished.
syn: poise, assurance *ant*: awkwardness

9. **bandy** (băn´ dē) *verb* to give and take quickly in conversation; to toss back and forth
"Let's not *bandy* words," the woman told her son. "Just tell me what happened."
syn: exchange (words)

10. **bane** (bān) *noun* the cause of ruin, harm or distress
As he passed out midterm grades, the teacher woefully told the students, "You'll be the *bane* of me yet."
syn: scourge *ant*: aid, benefit

Exercise I Words in Context

Fill in the blanks with the correct vocabulary words needed to complete the sentences.

animate **bane** **aphorism** **amalgamates** **bandies** **antiquated**

A. The novel *Frankenstein* is about a scientist named Victor Frankenstein, who devotes his life to studying the theories of ancient philosophers that Victor's contemporaries say are too ______________ to be of any modern use. Nevertheless, it is Victor's dream to ______________ non-living matter and create a living being, so he continues his studies.

B. After discovering the secret of life, Victor ______________ about the idea of whether or not to create a living being. Finally, he settles the question with the ______________, "Nothing ventured, nothing gained."

C. He takes various human parts and ______________ them into one gigantic body, which he brings to life. Victor thinks this achievement will bring him glory, but it turns out to be the ______________ of his existence.

anthropomorphic **aplomb** **anachronism** **ambidextrous**

D. Most movies portray Victor Frankenstein as a mad scientist of the nineteenth century, but this is an ______________, as the book was written early in the 1800s and is actually set some time in the mid-eighteenth century.

E. Many left-handed people have become ______________ when forced to adapt to a right-handed world.

F. In the mythologies of ancient Greece and Rome, we say that the gods are ______________ because they possess the characteristics and behaviors of humans.

G. Before reading the book *How to Win Friends and Influence People*, I was terribly shy; but afterwards, I handled social situations with great ______________.

Exercise II Roots, Prefixes, and Suffixes

Study the entries and answer the questions that follow.

The root *chroma* means "color."
The prefix *mono–* means "one."
The prefix *poly–* means "many."

1. Without using a dictionary, try to define the following words:

polychromatic	monotonous
monochromatic	monorail
polygon	monomania

2. *Morphology* is the study of forms. Animals that take on many forms during their life cycles are called ________________.

3. List as many words as you can think of which contain the root *chroma*, the prefix *poly–*, or the prefix *mono–*.

Exercise III Usage Inferences

Choose the answer that best fits the situation.

1. A good example of *anthropomorphism* may be found in
   A. newspaper articles.
   B. animated cartoons.
   C. popular sports.
   D. television talk shows.

2. An idea that some people find *antiquated* is
   A. the survival of the fittest.
   B. a woman's place is only in the home.
   C. the way to a man's heart is through his stomach.
   D. two wrongs do not make a right.

3. Who is the least likely to *bandy* words?
   A. a politician
   B. a comedian
   C. a salesman
   D. a scientist

Exercise IV Reading Comprehension

Read the selection and answer the questions.

The Industrial Revolution that took place in England between 1750 and 1825 was to change the life of Western Europe fundamentally. These changes would be most marked in the political and social life of the mass of mankind. For example, as a group, the peasants moved or were forced off the farms and into burgeoning cities. There, people provided the cheap labor that kept the wheels of industry rolling. As the people crowded into the cities, life in the city became a matter of survival. Housing conditions were deplorable; overcrowding and unsanitary conditions were the norm. The quality of life plummeted. Because of the terrible social conditions in which the volatile mass of people lived, they were ripe to be led into some political movement. Heretofore, the common man had little political voice, but it had never seemed to matter to him. Given the new conditions, however, the common man's indifference to politics would not last.

1. The main idea in this selection is that
   A. people provided the cheap labor that propelled the industrial revolution forward.
   B. the Industrial Revolution made a profound change in the life of Western Europe.
   C. the quality of life in Western Europe plummeted as a result of the Industrial Revolution.
   D. the Industrial Revolution made Western Europe a mighty political and economic power.

2. The writer states or implies that
   A. the rich people were the only ones with political power up until this time.
   B. life in the city, as hard as it was for the peasants, was preferable to life in the country.
   C. an armed revolution was bound to follow the Industrial Revolution.
   D. the Industrial Revolution made the common man economically self-sufficient, although conditions were hard.

3. In this writer's opinion, it appears that the Industrial Revolution
   A. brought wealth to the common man.
   B. brought a good deal of suffering to the common man.
   C. turned England into a second-rate power.
   D. brought prosperity to everyone in the country.

4. From this article, we might infer that the Industrial Revolution
   A. brought material wealth to a few but misery for many.
   B. created slums in many cities.
   C. made the poor, working people more class conscious.
   D. All of the above are correct.

Lesson Three

1. **beget** (bĭ gĕt´) *verb* to produce; to be the parent of
Hatred *begets* more hatred.
syn: cause, create, bring

2. **begrudge** (bĭ grŭj´) *verb* to resent another's success; to give with reluctance
The old miser *begrudged* every cent he paid to the caretaker.
syn: envy

3. **belated** (bĭ lā´ tĭd) *adj.* delayed
Joan sent a *belated* birthday card to her sister.
syn: tardy; late *ant*: timely

4. **beleaguer** (bĭ lē´ gər) *verb* to besiege by encircling (as with an army); to harass
The picnickers were *beleaguered* with pesky ants and flies.
syn: surround; annoy

5. **benediction** (bĕn ĭ dĭk´ shən) *noun* a blessing
We bowed our heads for the *benediction* before singing the closing hymn.
ant: curse, malediction

6. **beneficiary** (bĕn ə fĭsh´ ē ĕr ē) *noun* one who receives benefits
John was the sole *beneficiary* of his Uncle Martin's vast estate.

7. **berate** (bĭ rāt´) *verb* to scold or rebuke severely and at length
The coach *berated* the three players for arriving late.
syn: reprimand *ant*: praise

8. **berserk** (bər zûrk´) *adj.* showing reckless behavior or lack of control
My father went a little *berserk* when I told him I had put a dent in his new car.
syn: frenzied, crazed

9. **bias** (bī´ əs) *noun* a prejudiced view (either for or against) that inhibits impartial judgment
The jurors were instructed to review the facts without *bias*.
syn: favor *ant*: impartiality, objectivity

10. **bibliophile** (bĭb´ lē ə fīl) *noun* a lover of books
Having been a *bibliophile* since childhood, Mrs. Duncan was the perfect librarian.

Exercise I Words in Context

Fill in the blanks with the correct vocabulary words needed to complete the sentences.

benediction **bibliophiles** **beneficiaries** **begets**

A. During the ceremony, the excited ______________ listened patiently to the ______________ before the doors of the new library opened for the first time.

B. Unequal distribution of assets ______________ resentment and disagreements among ______________, so it's important to be fair to everyone when creating a will.

berserk **berated** **begrudge** **bias** **beleaguered** **belated**

C. When Callie finished her song, a large section of people in the audience went ______________, applauding wildly and shouting that she was the best in the competition. They were clearly showing a ______________ toward the hometown favorite.

D. I don't really mind paying a lot to see my favorite band in concert, but I do ______________ the ridiculous fees I have to pay the ticket agency. However, I feel bad for the ______________ customer service representatives who get ______________ for it by people who want to take their anger out on someone.

E. I was out of town when Linda's father died, so when I returned, I called Linda to offer my ______________ condolences.

Exercise II Roots, Prefixes, and Suffixes

Study the entries and answer the questions that follow.

The prefix *biblo–* means "book."
The root *voc/vox* means "call."
The root *mort* means "death."

1. Without using a dictionary, try to define the following words:
   bibliography vocation
   biblical vociferous
   mortician mortuary

2. List as many words as you can think of that contain the roots *mort*, *voc/vox,* and the prefix *biblio–*.

Exercise III Usage Inferences

Choose the answer that best fits the situation.

1. A *benediction* is most frequently said in a
   A. church.
   B. school.
   C. hospital.
   D. college.

2. One is most likely to *begrudge* an enemy's
   A. failures.
   B. successes.
   C. lies.
   D. troubles.

3. Someone who is *berserk* is likely to demonstrate
   A. a lack of self-control.
   B. a keen intellect.
   C. an allergic reaction.
   D. an unusual skill.

Exercise IV Reading Comprehension

Read the selection and answer the questions.

Children who are regularly spanked or beaten by their parents run a higher risk of becoming delinquents, or even killers, than children who are not physically punished. This is a conclusion drawn by sociologist Murray Straus. Straus believes that the research indicates that there is a link between corporal punishment and homicide.

Straus, an expert on family violence, states: "I found that the more parents spank, the higher the homicide rate." Straus, who heads his university's family research laboratory, has published twelve books.

Children who receive physical punishment will not necessarily grow up to be criminals, but they may be at increased risk for violent behavior. His research, published in the journal, *Social Problems*, compared homicide rates and the use of corporal punishment among United States and ten European nations. Straus also cited research findings indicating that parents who spank frequently are more likely to abuse their children in other ways.

"It is difficult to establish a direct cause-and-effect relationship between spanking and violence because parents tend to spank children who are already aggressive and violent," he said. Most attending the conference would agree that severe physical punishment has damaging long-term effects on children.

1. The phrase that best describes the topic of this piece is
   A. violence in the home.
   B. a more violent society.
   C. the dangers of spanking.
   D. parents and children.

2. The main idea of this piece is
   A. parents who spank their children are more likely to abuse their children in other ways, than parents who do not spank.
   B. parents who received large amounts of physical punishment as a child are more likely to abuse their own children than those who didn't.
   C. spanking and physical abuse may turn children into delinquents.
   D. Europeans physically punish children less than Americans do.

3. The article suggests or states that
   A. children who are aggressive and violent are spanked no more often than children who are not.
   B. severe physical punishment has long-term effects on children.
   C. more murders are committed in the United States than in Europe.
   D. Both A and B are correct.

4. The author gathered some of the facts he used to arrive at his conclusions by
   A. talking with murderers.
   B. sitting down and thinking a long time about it.
   C. comparing the use of corporal punishment in the U.S. with that of other countries.
   D. talking with police, killers, and judges.

Lesson Four

1. **bilk** (bĭlk) *verb* to cheat or swindle; to thwart or frustrate
The con artists tried to *bilk* the elderly homeowner by charging him for work he never authorized.
syn: defraud, elude

2. **blatant** (blāt´ nt) *adj.* offensively noisy; obvious, too conspicuous
His *blatant* efforts to get the girl's attention were ineffective.
syn: vociferous

3. **blight** (blīt) *noun* anything that destroys, prevents growth, or causes devaluation
My tomato plants were all affected with *blight,* and they died despite my efforts to save them.
syn: disease

4. **cache** (kăsh) *noun* a hiding place; or things hidden, usually valuables
They used a hole in a hollow tree, known to only the three of them, as their *cache.*

5. **cadaverous** (kə dăv´ ər əs) *adj.* of or like a corpse; pale, gaunt, thin
The old pirate's *cadaverous* face made the young sailor tremble involuntarily.
syn: ghastly *ant:* robust, healthy

6. **calumny** (kăl´ əm nē) *noun* a false and malicious accusation
The politician said that he was retiring from public life because he could no longer stand the *calumnies* spoken against him by his rivals.
syn: slander, trickery

7. **careen** (kə rēn´) *verb* to lean sideways; to lurch from side to side while in motion
The torrential winds caused the ship to *careen* violently.
syn: tilt, lurch

8. **caricature** (kăr´ ĭ kə choor) *noun* an exaggerated portrayal of one's features
In his political cartoons, the artist exaggerates a prominent feature of the person in order to make the *caricature* easily recognizable.
syn: mockery

9. **carnage** (kär´ nĭj) *noun* a bloody and extensive slaughter
It was a pointless war that that didn't resolve anything and resulted only in the *carnage* of many innocent civilians.
syn: massacre

10. **carp** (kärp) *verb* to complain or to find fault in a petty or nagging way
One reason you are not very popular is that you *carp* about every little thing.
syn: nag, grouse *ant:* praise, laud

Exercise I Words in Context

Fill in the blanks with the correct vocabulary words needed to complete the sentences.

careen	**caricature**	**carp**	**bilked**	**cadaverous**

A. During his illness, old Mr. Johnson was so pale that he looked absolutely ________________. His weight loss made his hollow cheeks and deep-set eyes even more so, and he looked like a skeletal ________________ of himself. He was so weak that when he tried to walk, he ________________ down the hallway, and had to be helped back to his bed.

B. Although the coach generally did not like to ________________ about his players' poor performances when they lost, he did spend forty minutes after this game pointing out their shortcomings.

C. The corrupt stockbroker had ________________ investors out of millions of dollars before he was caught when a client became suspicious of him.

cache	**carnage**	**blight**	**blatant**	**calumny**

D. After the shelling stopped, the battlefield was a scene of mutilation and ________________.

E. He said that he didn't mind criticism, but that he objected strenuously to the ________________ distortions and ________________ spread by his opponent.

F. Most of the elm trees in America were destroyed by a ________________ known as Dutch elm disease.

G. Before banks became secure, people used to hide their life savings in a ________________ underneath their mattresses.

Exercise II Roots, Prefixes, and Suffixes

Study the entries and answer the questions that follow.

The root *term* means "end." The root *ver* means "true."

1. Without using a dictionary, try to define the following words:
   terminal verify
   terminate verity
   exterminate

2. The end of the bus route is at the city's largest ______________.

3. List as many words as you can think of that contain the roots *term* or *ver.*

Exercise III Usage Inferences

Choose the answer that best fits the situation.

1. *Carnage* is most likely to occur
   A. at a ball game.
   B. an economic crisis.
   C. during a war.
   D. after a war ends.

2. At a party, one who *carps* frequently would most likely
   A. be very popular.
   B. be very interesting.
   C. be very dull.
   D. be avoided by others.

3. The most likely place to see a *cadaver* is
   A. in a classroom.
   B. in a morgue.
   C. at a dance.
   D. at a football game.

Exercise IV Reading Comprehension

Read the selection and answer the questions.

If the Greek classics are to be read with any benefit by modern men, they must be read as the work of men like ourselves. Regard must be had to their traditions, their opportunities, and their limitations. There is a disposition to exaggeration in all human admiration; most of our classical texts are very much mangled, and all were originally the work of human beings in difficulties, living in a time of such darkness and narrowness of outlook as makes our own age by comparison a period of dazzling illumination. What we shall lose in reverence by this familiar treatment, we shall gain in sympathy for that group of troubled, uncertain, and very modern minds. The Athenian writers were, indeed, the first of modern men. They were discussing questions that we still discuss; they began to struggle with the great problems that confront us today. Their writings are our dawn.

H. G. Wells

1. In this selection, the author's main point is that
   A. the Greeks had their problems, too.
   B. the ancient Greek writers were people just like us.
   C. reading the Greek classics can benefit modern man.
   D. the Greeks lived in an age of darkness and uncertainty.

2. The author states or implies that modern man
   A. is not as strong as the ancients were.
   B. has an exaggerated admiration for the ancient writers.
   C. has underrated the ancient writers.
   D. has little to learn from reading the works of ancient writers.

3. It appears that this writer
   A. greatly admires the ancient writers.
   B. has little respect for the ancient writers.
   C. thinks that we have to recognize our common humanity with the ancients.
   D. Both A and C are correct.

4. The selection states or implies that
   A. our own age, by comparison, is more intellectually enlightened than ancient times.
   B. the classics have little to say to modern man.
   C. everything that needs to be said about life has already been said by the ancients.
   D. the classics come to us in pure and uncorrupted versions.

Lesson Five

1. **catalyst** (kăt´ l ĭst) *noun* a person, thing, or agent that speeds up or stimulates a result, reaction, or change
A slight tap from the riding crop was all the *catalyst* the race horse needed to put on speed and leave the others behind.

2. **catholic** (kăth´ ə lĭk) *adj.* universal; wide-ranging
His interests were so *catholic* that he could talk knowledgeably on almost any subject.
syn: broad, liberal *ant*: provincial, limited, parochial

3. **cavort** (kə vôrt´) *verb* to leap about in a lively manner; romp
The stray puppy began to *cavort* with the children on the playground.
syn: frolic, prance, caper

4. **chafe** (chāf) *verb* to irritate as if by friction or rubbing
The stinging wind began to *chafe* our faces as we struggled through the storm.
syn: annoy, abrade *ant*: soothe

5. **charisma** (kə rĭz´ mə) noun a great appeal or attraction for others; personal magnetism
Although the candidate was very handsome and had a great deal of *charisma*, he had absolutely no knowledge about the issues that concerned people the most.
syn: allure, charm

6. **chauvinist** (shō´ və nĭst) *noun* a person who believes in the superiority of his or her country, race, gender, etc.
Although he did not dislike women, he certainly was a male *chauvinist* and had a hard time treating females as equals.

7. **chicanery** (shĭ kā´ nə r ē) *noun* trickery; the use of cleverness to deceive or evade
The district attorney was accused of *chicanery* by the defense counsel.
syn: ruse *ant*: honesty

8. **choleric** (kŏl âr´ ĭk) *adj.* easily angered
He was a *choleric* man whose temper was bound to get him in trouble.
syn: quick-tempered, irascible, irritable *ant*: phlegmatic, impassive

9. **dally** (dăl´ ē) *verb* to waste time; dawdle
We *dallied* with the idea of a cruise but eventually decided to fly to Rio.
syn: linger, toy *ant*: hasten, hurry

10. **dastardly** (dăs´ tərd lē) *adj.* mean and cowardly
Only a *dastardly* person would poison someone's pet dog.
syn: malicious

Exercise I Words in Context

Fill in the blanks with the correct vocabulary words needed to complete the sentences.

dastardly **chicanery** **charisma** **chauvinist** **catholic**

A. In my favorite childhood TV show, the ______________ villain planned to take over the world and used ______________ to fool people and avoid being captured, but the superhero always foiled him in the end.

B. It is not necessary to have a liberal upbringing to be ______________ in one's views.

C. Although he had a lot of ______________, the disrespectful way he talked to women earned him the label of a male ______________, and no one would go out him.

choleric **catalyst** **chafed** **cavort** **dally**

D. Daria went outside to ______________ in the snow with the other children. Later, she returned home crying because her wool socks had ______________ her feet.

E. Sondra would always ______________ at the mall with her friends on the weekends instead of doing something more constructive with her time.

F. In chemistry, heat is often used as a ______________; it will speed up the reaction without changing the results.

G. Olivia seemed nice at first, but her ______________ personality soon became apparent when I saw her screaming at her best friends.

Exercise II Roots, Prefixes, and Suffixes

Study the entries and answer the questions that follow.

The root *corp* means "body."
The prefix *inter–* means "between" or "among."

The root *rupt* means "break."

1. Without using a dictionary, try to define the following words:

   corporal
   corporation
   incorporate

   interrupt
   erupt
   corrupt

2. Because he ignored the pain for too long, they had to rush him to the hospital with a ________________ appendix.

3. List as many words as you can think of that contain the prefix *inter–* or the roots *corp* and *rupt*.

Exercise III Usage Inferences

Choose the answer that best fits the situation.

1. A *choleric* person would probably not make a good
   A. computer programmer.
   B. brick layer.
   C. real estate agent.
   D. book editor.

2. A *dastardly* student is likely to be
   A. popular with his classmates.
   B. unpopular with teachers.
   C. liked by everyone.
   D. despised by everyone.

3. A person must be most alert for *chicanery* in
   A. a handbook for new students.
   B. a training manual for soldiers.
   C. an installment sales contract.
   D. a court summons.

Exercise IV Reading Comprehension

Read the selection and answer the questions.

[The Greek philosophers] began an inquiry, and they arrived at no solutions. We cannot pretend today that we have arrived at solutions to most of the questions they asked. The mind of the Hebrews, as we have already shown, awoke suddenly to the endless miseries and disorders of life, saw that these miseries and disorders were largely due to the lawless acts of men, and concluded that salvation could come only through subduing ourselves to the service of the one God who rules heaven and earth. The Greek, rising to the same perception, was not prepared with the same idea of a patriarchal deity; he lived in a world in which there was not God but the gods; if perhaps he felt that the gods themselves were limited, then he thought of Fate behind them, cold and impersonal. So he put his problem in the form of an inquiry as to what was right living, without any definite correlation of the right-living man with the will of God.

H. G. Wells

1. In this selection, the author essentially wishes to
   A. praise the Hebrews and condemn the Greeks.
   B. praise the Greeks and condemn the Hebrews.
   C. prove or disprove the existence of an almighty being.
   D. discuss how both groups of ancients viewed man's existence.

2. Wells, who is sometimes called the "Father of Science Fiction," demonstrates in this selection
   A. a desire to predict the future.
   B. a bitter view of man's existence.
   C. a keen grasp of ancient history.
   D. a curiosity regarding the existence of God.

3. The author states or implies that
   A. the Greeks were superior to the Hebrews in intellectual activities.
   B. the Hebrews posited a God and, thereby, took the easy answer.
   C. the Greeks raised questions but failed to come up with answers because they stopped trying.
   D. the questions raised by the ancients are questions that modern man is still trying to answer.

4. The author states or implies that the
   A. Hebrews saw the senselessness of life and posited the existence of a God who could bring about man's salvation.
   B. Greeks also saw the senselessness of life but came up with the conclusion that man, not God, is in charge of his own fate.
   C. raising of questions about life and its meaning answers few questions but causes many problems.
   D. idea of a patriarchal deity, who was both cold and impersonal, was arrived at by both the Hebrews and Greeks, but by different paths.

Lesson Six

1. **daub** (dôb) *verb* to paint coarsely or unskillfully
Bright colors were *daubed* randomly over the artist's easel.
syn: smear

2. **daunt** (dônt) *verb* to make afraid or discouraged
The explorers were not *daunted* by the high waves and bitter cold; they continued to sail toward the island.
syn: dismay, intimidate *ant*: encourage

3. **dawdle** (dôd´ l) *verb* to waste time
"Don't *dawdle* children," the governess called up the stairs. "We must hurry."
syn: tarry, loiter *ant*: hasten, expedite

4. **debonair** (dĕb ə nâr´) *adj.* carefree and self-confident; elegant and gracious
I expected to see an awkward young man, so I was quite surprised to see a *debonair* gentleman instead.
syn: charming, suave *ant*: gauche, awkward

5. **decadence** (dek´ ə dəns) *noun* moral deterioration
It has often been suggested that the fall of Rome was a result of its *decadence.*
syn: decay, decline *ant*: progress

6. **declaim** (dĭ klām´) *verb* to speak in a dramatic, pompous, or blustering manner
The judge told the actor to answer the questions simply and leave his *declaiming* for the stage.
syn: orate, harangue *ant*: whisper

7. **defunct** (dĭ fŭngkt) *adj.* no longer in existence
I discovered too late that the bargain stock I had purchased was for a *defunct* corporation.

8. **deify** (dē´ ə fī) *verb* to make a god of; to look upon or worship as a god
He had *deified* her and was crushed when she turned out to be a mere human like the rest of us.
syn: idolize, adore, exalt *ant*: abhor, detest

9. **delete** (dĭ lēt´) *verb* to take out; cross out
Delete the second sentence; you already made your point, and the repetition only weakens your argument.
syn: erase, wipe out *ant*: include, add

10. **delude** (dĭ lo͞od´) *verb* to mislead; to fool
We were *deluded* into thinking we could trust the smooth-talking salesman.
syn: deceive

Exercise I Words in Context

Fill in the blanks with the correct vocabulary words needed to complete the sentences.

delete	**deluded**	**declaimed**	**deify**	**decadence**

A. Barbara always ______________ herself into thinking that winning the lottery would solve all her problems.

B. Many modern websites celebrate the ______________ and affluence of celebrities, but I read something that encourages people to live a simple life rather than ______________ wealth.

C. In his speech, the mayor ______________ against the lawlessness he observed in his city.

D. The journalist's editor told her to ______________ any comments that might make the article appear biased.

daunt	**dawdle**	**debonair**	**defunct**	**daub**

E. It's funny to watch how little children ______________ on the way to school. Even rainy weather does not ______________ their enthusiasm.

F. After one last ______________, the artist stood back and let Mr. Johnson look at the picture. Mr. Johnson was surprised to see not the ______________ gentleman he thought he was, but rather a painting of a tired, bedraggled businessman.

G. As a result of the popularity of the computer, companies that had made only typewriters are now ______________.

Exercise II Roots, Prefixes, and Suffixes

Study the entries and answer the questions that follow.

The root *poten* means "power." The prefix *psych–* means "mind."

A. Without using a dictionary, try to define the following words:

potential	psychological
potent	psycho-drama
potentate	psyche

B. People who can read minds and predict the future are said to have ______________ power.

C. List as many words as you can think of that contain the root *poten* or the prefix *psych–*.

Exercise III Usage Inferences

Choose the answer that best fits the situation.

1. The person you would least likely expect to *delude* you is
   A. an auto mechanic.
   B. a salesman.
   C. a reporter.
   D. a college professor.

2. That which most likely would make a company *defunct* would be
   A. a large labor pool.
   B. a surplus of capital.
   C. advancing technology.
   D. advanced management skills.

3. Someone who is *undaunted* by a situation would
   A. give up completely.
   B. complain loudly.
   C. put off handling it.
   D. try to overcome it.

Exercise IV Reading Comprehension

Read the selection and answer the questions.

A study funded by the Carnegie Corporation concluded that a majority of workers in the United States face a lifetime of low-paying jobs. As a result, this country will lose the global economic fight to other nations unless some changes are made in the training of the average worker. The report states: "What we are facing is an economic cliff of sorts. Unfortunately, the frontline working people of America are about to fall off that cliff."

The report goes on to say: "Seventy percent of the work force—the clerks, secretaries, machinists, drivers, farm workers, and other non college-educated frontline workers—will see their dreams slip away unless society invests far more in improving their skills in school and on the job."

The report—"America's Choice: high skills or low wages!"—calls on business, schools and government to totally overhaul the "haphazard, incoherent and bureaucratic" system of job training now in operation.

The report recommends that all students be required to work toward a "Certificate of Initial Mastery." This certificate would certify high levels of competence in math, English, and other job basics. Students would demonstrate their skills through performing specific tasks rather than taking standardized tests.

1. The main point in this selection is that
   A. other countries are doing a better job training workers than we are.
   B. the present system of training workers in the United States is inadequate.
   C. the standard of living for the average American worker is falling.
   D. U.S. schools need to set higher standards for all students.

2. The tone of this piece is one of
   A. quiet thoughtfulness.
   B. angry denunciation.
   C. concern or alarm.
   D. sad reflection.

3. The selection states or implies that if action isn't taken,
   A. the U.S. will become an economically inferior country.
   B. the U.S. worker will fall further and further behind.
   C. the U.S. educational system, already behind other nations, will fall even further behind.
   D. All of the above are correct.

4. The selection states or implies that the way to change the situation is
   A. to provide more technical education to non-college-bound students.
   B. to follow Europe's lead and set up a better apprenticeship program.
   C. to hold all students to higher standards of performance.
   D. All of the above are correct.

Lesson Seven

1. **deluge** (dĕl´ yōōj) *noun* a flood; downpour; an overwhelming rush or amount
The new amusement park had a *deluge* of visitors on opening day.
syn: torrent, inundation

2. **demented** (dĭ mĕn´ tĭd) *adj.* mentally ill; insane
After observing his *demented* behavior for a few minutes, we decided to call the doctor.
syn: deranged *ant*: sane, balanced

3. **demise** (dĭ mīz´) *noun* death; a ceasing of existance
Upon her Uncle Ian's *demise*, Mary was to receive his property.
syn: termination, conclusion

4. **denigrate** (dĕn´ ĭ grāt) *verb* to ruin the reputation of; speak ill of
His opponent's slanderous remarks could not *denigrate* the fine work done by Senator Owens.
syn: blacken, defame *ant*: praise, promote

5. **denizen** (dĕn´ ĭ zən) *noun* an occupant; inhabitant
The Greek god Hades ruled over the *denizens* of the underworld.
syn: inhabitant, resident

6. **deplete** (dĭ plēt´) *verb* to use up gradually
After we had *depleted* our meager food supply, we decided it was time to come out of hiding.
syn: empty, exhaust *ant*: replenish

7. **desecrate** (dĕs´ ĭ krāt) *verb* to damage a holy place; to treat with irreverence
The small church had been *desecrated* by vandals.
syn: profane *ant*: consecrate

8. **desist** (dĭ sĭst´) *verb* to stop; cease
After many long hours, the rescue crew was told to *desist* in its futile efforts to recover the wreckage.
syn: end, halt *ant*: start, proceed

9. **desolate** (dĕs´ ə lĭt) *adj.* lonely; forlorn; uninhabited; barren
The small raft washed ashore on a *desolate* island many miles from the mainland.
syn: dismal, wretched *ant*: populous, crowded

10. **despot** (dĕs´ pət) *noun* a ruler with absolute power; a dictator
Stalin was a cruel *despot* who was responsible for the deaths of a huge number of people.
syn: autocrat, tyrant

Exercise I Words in Context

Fill in the blanks with the correct vocabulary words needed to complete the sentences.

demise **demented** **desecrated** **despot** **denizens**

A. When I visited the ancient monuments, I was saddened to see that they had been ______________ by graffiti. When I spoke to the ______________ of the town, they said the police had arrested someone whose ______________ ranting clearly connected him to the crime.

B. Upon the ______________ of the tyrannical ______________, leadership passed to his eldest son, who proved to be a fair and compassionate ruler.

desolate **deluge** **desist** **denigrated** **deplete**

C. The scandal ______________ his reputation, and he lost many supporters because of it. He felt ______________ and hopeless until he was able to prove he had not been involved in the situation.

D. During the drought, some people continued to ______________ the water supply by watering their lawns, which forced the mayor to issue an order to ______________ from non-essential water use until further notice. Fortunately, the area received a ______________ of rain before the situation became critical.

Exercise II Roots, Prefixes, and Suffixes

Study the entries and answer the questions that follow.

The prefix *liber–* means "free." The root *soph* means "wisdom."

1. Without using a dictionary, try to define the following words:

philosophy liberty
sophomore liberate
sophist liberal

2. The mother had wanted to name her baby girl Agnes, but the father, hoping the girl would grow to be wise, named her ______________.

3. List as many words as you can think of that contain the prefix *liber–* or the root *soph*.

Exercise III Usage Inferences

Choose the answer that best fits the situation.

1. A *denizen* of the sea would most likely
   A. dislike it.
   B. be afraid of it.
   C. live in it.
   D. study it.

2. A *deluge* may be caused by
   A. hard economic times.
   B. a driver's carelessness.
   C. freezing temperatures.
   D. a tropical storm.

3. The *demise* of a business would probably be welcome news to
   A. the company's stockholders.
   B. the president of the company.
   C. customers of the business.
   D. the company's most bitter competitor.

Exercise IV Reading Comprehension

Read the selection and answer the questions.

One great idea on which all tragedy builds is the idea of the continuity of human life. The one thing a man cannot do is exactly what all modern artists and free lovers are always trying to do. He cannot cut his life up into separate sections. The case of the modern claim for freedom in love is the first and most obvious that occurs to the mind; therefore, I use it for this purpose of illustration. You cannot have an idyll with Maria and an episode with Jane; there is no such thing as an episode. There is no such thing as an idyll. It is idle to talk about abolishing the tragedy of marriage when you cannot abolish the tragedy of sex. Every flirtation is a marriage; it is a marriage in this frightful sense: that it is irrevocable. I have taken this case of sexual relations as one out of a hundred; but of any case in human life the thing is true. The basis of all tragedy is that man lives a coherent and continuous life. It is only a worm that you can cut in two and leave the severed parts still alive. You can cut a worm up into episodes and they are still living episodes. You can cut a worm up into idylls and they are quite brisk and lively idylls. You can do all this to him precisely because he is a worm. You cannot cut a man up and leave him kicking, precisely because he is a man. We know this because man even in his lowest and darkest manifestation has always this characteristic of physical and psychological unity. His identity continues long enough to see the end of many of his own acts; he cannot be cut off from his past with a hatchet; as he sows so shall he reap.

G. K. Chesterton

1. The main idea of this selection is that
   A. tragedy is inevitable in a man's life.
   B. man for all his pretensions is still, like a worm, only an animal.
   C. marriage may begin with an innocent flirtation but requires a lifelong commitment.
   D. man lives life in a continuity that cannot be broken up into separate episodes.

2. The writer compares and contrasts the life of man to
   A. that of a worm.
   B. a bad play.
   C. a successful marriage.
   D. a tragedy.

3. An idea that is *not* stated or implied in this selection is
   A. a man's life cannot be cut up into segments.
   B. the basis of all tragedy is that man lives a continuous life.
   C. that all true love stories end in death.
   D. each act in a man's life contributes to the whole life.

4. We might infer that the writer believes that
   A. most marriages are unhappy ones.
   B. marriage is too constricting for a man.
   C. infidelity is bound to occur in a marriage.
   D. infidelity is bad for a marriage.

VOCABULARY for the College Bound

Lesson Eight

1. **edifice** (ĕd´ ə fĭs) *noun* a large, elaborate structure; an imposing building
The palace was not just a place to live; it was an *edifice* meant to excite the envy of the other princes.
syn: building

2. **educe** (ĭ dōōs´) *verb* to draw or bring out
The lawyer tried to *educe* a response from the witness.
syn: elicit *ant*: suppress

3. **eerie** (ēr´ ē) *adj.* mysterious; strange; frightening
We had an *eerie* feeling about entering the deserted old house at night.
syn: weird *ant*: common, ordinary

4. **efface** (ĭ fās´) *verb* to obliterate; to wipe out
It appeared that he had tried to *efface* her very memory by burning all her pictures.
syn: erase *ant*: enshrine

5. **effrontery** (ĭ frŭn´ tə rē) *noun* unashamed boldness
The thief had the *effrontery* to demand a reward for returning the money he had stolen.
syn: presumptuousness, impudence, audacity

6. **effusive** (ĭ fyōō´ sĭv) *adj.* overly demonstrative; overflowing
She was so *effusive* that everyone stared at us, and I was sorry that I agreed to meet her in a public place.
syn: gushing *ant*: reserved, restrained

7. **egalitarian** (ĭ gal ĭ ter´ ē ən) *adj.* belief in the equality of all people
The equal rights amendment for women was founded on *egalitarian* principles.
ant: elitist

8. **egress** (ē´ grĕs) *noun* a way out; the right or act of going out
The deed to the property did not specify that the buyer had rights of ingress and *egress* over the adjoining land.
syn: exit *ant*: ingress, entrance

9. **elated** (ĭ lā´ tĭd) *adj.* to be in high spirits; exultantly proud and joyful
We were *elated* at the prospects of a Caribbean cruise.
syn: overjoyed *ant*: depressed

10. **elite** (ə lēt´) *noun* the choice or best of a group
An *elite* army group, specially trained in anti-terrorist tactics, stormed the building.
ant: common, multitude

Exercise I Words in Context

Fill in the blanks with the correct vocabulary words needed to complete the sentences.

elite **egress** **efface** **effrontery** **eerie** **edifice**

A. The architect had worked hard to design an elaborate ______________ that met the specifications of his client who was an ______________ athlete. After approving the plans, the client had the ______________ to blame the architect for not including an ______________ that led directly to the tennis court, a feature the client had not originally asked for.

B. Dan has never been able to ______________ the memory of the sounds he heard when he toured the historic battlefield. They sounded like the ______________ voices of soldiers who had died in battle.

elated **egalitarian** **educe** **effusive**

C. Most parents in the district were ______________ when the school board adopted an ______________ policy regarding females playing on traditionally male sports teams.

D. Some teenagers are embarrassed by the ______________ greetings they receive from older relatives.

E. No matter how I phrased the question, I could not ______________ the correct answer from the class.

Exercise II Roots, Prefixes, and Suffixes

Study the entries and answer the questions that follow.

The root *phon* means "sound." The prefix *tele–* means "distance."

1. Without using a dictionary, try to define the following words:
   telephone telegraph
   television telepathy
   polyphonic symphony

2. The study of the sounds of letters, letter groups, and words used to teach children to read is called ______________.

3. List as many words as you can think of that contain the root *phon* or the prefix *tele–*.

Exercise III Usage Inferences

Choose the answer that best fits the situation.

1. Which of the following would be most likely described as an *edifice*?
   A. the Statue of Liberty
   B. the Empire State Building
   C. Abraham Lincoln's birthplace
   D. the Union Pacific Railroad

2. People would most likely look for and find an *egress*
   A. in a theater.
   B. in a bird refuge.
   C. at the beach.
   D. in a book.

3. Of the following, the person most likely to be *effusive* is
   A. a timid child.
   B. a police officer.
   C. a bubbly, teenage girl.
   D. an elderly man.

Exercise IV Reading Comprehension

Read the selection and answer the questions.

The South accounts for about a third of the crimes reported in the United States and nearly 60 percent of the felony convictions in state courts, the Justice Department says.

People arrested on felony charges in the South are more likely to be convicted than those arrested elsewhere in the United States, according to a study made public by the department's Bureau of Justice Statistics.

For every 1,000 felony arrests in the South, there were 143 convictions, the department said. In contrast, the annual conviction rates were 58 per 1,000 felony arrests in the West, 60 in the Northeast, and 78 in the Midwest. High conviction rates were generally found in less populated areas, the bureau reports.

Counties with fewer than 100,000 people throughout the United States had about a sixth of the reported crime, but accounted for more than two-thirds of the nation's felony convictions, the study said. "We were surprised to find out how much more likely offenders in small counties are to be arrested and prosecuted for felonies than are those in large counties," said Steven Schlosinger, director of the bureau.

One possible explanation, he said, is that crime in urban areas is so serious and frequent that law-enforcement officials are more selective about investigation and prosecution.

1. The best title for this article is
   A. South is Crime Capital of the Country.
   B. South Leads Nation in Conviction Rate.
   C. Harsh Justice in the South.
   D. More Crime in City Than in County.

2. This article states or implies that
   A. proportionately more adults are arrested in the South than juveniles.
   B. crimes in less-populated areas are more thoroughly investigated than crimes in urban areas.
   C. there is a 40% chance you will be convicted if you are arrested for a crime in the South.
   D. the conviction rate in the Midwest is the highest at 78%.

3. The article also states or implies that
   A. today's cities are unsafe.
   B. the results of the study confirm everyone's earlier opinions.
   C. justice in the South is harsh and not always fair.
   D. because of the high volume of crime in urban areas, only the most serious are investigated.

4. The general tone of this article is one of
   A. condemnation and criticism.
   B. surprise and wonder.
   C. objective reporting.
   D. admiration and praise.

Lesson Nine

1. **elude** (ĭ lōōd´) *verb* to escape notice; to get away from
The fugitive was able to *elude* his pursuers by carefully covering his tracks.
syn: avoid, evade, lose

2. **embroil** (ĕm broil´) *verb* to draw into a conflict or fight
The committee was *embroiled* in a heated discussion over the new zoning ordinance.
syn: entangle

3. **emissary** (ĕm´ ĭ sĕr ē) *noun* one sent on a special mission to represent others
In those days there was no such thing as diplomatic immunity, and an *emissary* was often taken captive and killed.

4. **emit** (ĭ mĭt´) *verb* to send out; to give forth, as in sound
The geyser Old Faithful *emits* water on a regular basis.
syn: discharge, issue, utter

5. **enmity** (ĕn´ mĭ tē) *noun* deep-seated hostility, often mutual
There had always been a feeling of *enmity* between the two schools.
syn: hatred, antagonism *ant:* friendship

6. **ensue** (ĕn sōō´) *verb* to result from; to come after
Spontaneous applause *ensued* when the principal announced that school would be closed for two weeks for repairs.
syn: follow

7. **entice** (ĕn tīs´) *verb* to attract by offering reward or pleasure
I was *enticed* by the color and style of the gown, but the price was too high.
syn: tempt, lure *ant:* discourage

8. **entity** (ĕn´ tĭ tē) *noun* an independent being; a real and independent existence.
There was no evil *entity* stalking the graveyard; what frightened him was just fog blown by the wind.

9. **envisage** (ĕn vĭz´ ĭj) *verb* to form a mental picture
Jack should try to *envisage* how he will do the task before he begins it.
syn: imagine, visualize

10. **epigram** (ĕp´ ĭ grăm) *noun* a witty saying expressing a single thought or observation
The guest speaker used many *epigrams* to hold the attention of his audience.
syn: quip

11. **epitaph** (ĕp´ ĭ tăf) *noun* an inscription on a tombstone
The *epitaph* on the headstone was simple, but meaningful: "Husband, Father, Friend."

12. **equivocal** (ĭ kwĭv´ ə kəl) *adj* ambiguous; purposely vague
He never said "Yes" or "No." He always had to give an *equivocal* answer.
syn: uncertain, questionable *ant:* certain, definite

13. **eradicate** (ĭ răd´ ĭ kāt) *verb* to wipe out; destroy
The girl tried to *eradicate* the memory of the crash from her mind.
syn: erase, eliminate *ant:* add, create

14. **fabricate** (făb´ rĭ kāt) *verb* to make, to build; to make up something in order to deceive
We tried to *fabricate* a story our parents would believe.
syn: erect, invent

15. **facade** (fə säd´) *noun* a deceptive outward appearance; the front part of a building
Although Joan put on a cheerful *facade*, we knew she was heartbroken.

Exercise I Words in Context

Fill in the blanks with the correct vocabulary words needed to complete the sentences.

entices **facade** **enmity** **ensuing** **emissary** **elude**

A. The strikers sent a(n) ________________ to the corporate headquarters to see if the issues could be resolved without ________________ .

B. When the plywood ________________ of a medieval castle fell down during the play, the ________________ chaos was nearly as dramatic as the play itself.

C. The Venus flytrap ________________ its prey with a flower-like appearance and a small amount of nectar. Most insects cannot ________________ its quick and powerful leaves.

eradicate **fabricate** **embroiled** **envisage**

D. John was ________________ in a debate with several people at the meeting; they could not ________________ using solar energy as the sole source of power in the U.S., but he insisted it was possible.

E. "You cannot ________________ a wrong simply by saying you are sorry," said the minister. "If you ________________ stories about your neighbors, you must make amends."

epigrams **epitaph** **entity** **equivocal** **emit**

F. When the nuclear power plant began to ______________ an abnormal amount of radioactive material, the ______________ that owned it gave an ______________ answer when asked if the reactor would be shut down.

G. Although writer Oscar Wilde was famous for his clever ______________, the ______________ on his tombstone is a verse from his poem "The Ballad of Reading Gaol."

Exercise II Roots, Prefixes, and Suffixes

Study the entries and answer the questions that follow.

The root *multi* means "many."
The root *nov* means "new."
The root *nau* refers to ships, sailors, or the sea.
The root *pater/patri* refers to father.

1. A male leader of a family, or the male who rules a tribe is called a ______________. (Keep in mind that arch is a root meaning "to rule.") But one who loves his fatherland is called a ______________. If you talk down to someone as if you were the father and he the child, you would be said to be ______________ing him. That which you might expect to inherit from your father is your ______________.

2. Someone who is new at something, a sport for example, is called a ______________. If we make something old like new, we may be said to have ______________ it. And if we come up with a new idea, it is called an in______________.

3. An expedition taken by ship would most likely be called a ______________ expedition.

4. Give a literal meaning for as many of these words as you can.

multitude multifarious patricide

Exercise III Usage Inferences

Choose the answer that best fits the situation.

1. A person who is *equivocal* on a controversial topic
   A. has a strong opinion.
   B. is disinterested in it.
   C. is undecided about it.
   D. thinks he is right.

2. *Enmity* is most likely to be found between
   A. two close friends.
   B. a husband and wife.
   C. two strangers.
   D. two foes or opponents.

3. A new *facade* would most likely be found
   A. on an old building.
   B. in a parking lot.
   C. in a department store.
   D. in the pocket of a wealthy person.

Exercise IV Reading Comprehension

Read the selection and answer the questions

This preface is essential if we are to profit by the main meaning of *Macbeth*. For the play is so very great that it covers much more than it appears to cover; it will certainly survive our age as it has survived its own; it will certainly leave the twentieth century behind as calmly and completely as it has left the seventeenth century behind. Hence if we ask for the meaning of this classic we must necessarily ask the meaning for our own time. It might have another shade of meaning for another period of time. If, as is possible, there should be a barbaric return and if history is any kind of guide, it will destroy everything else before it destroys great literature. The high and civilized sadness of Virgil was enjoyed literally through the darkest instant of the Dark Ages. Long after a wealthier generation has destroyed Parliament, they will retain Shakespeare. Men will enjoy the greatest tragedy of Shakespeare even in the thick of the greatest tragedy of Europe.

C. K. Chesterton

1. The main idea in this selection is that the play *Macbeth*
   A. is Shakespeare's greatest play.
   B. may be interpreted differently by different centuries.
   C. has so much in it that it will be read for centuries to come.
   D. is even more popular than the works of the Latin writer Virgil.

2. It is stated or implied that
   A. many people miss the true genius of Shakespeare.
   B. different ages will interpret literature in different ways.
   C. of all Shakespeare's tragedies, *Macbeth* is the only good one.
   D. Both A and B are correct.

3. This writer appears to believe that
   A. the play *Macbeth* was unpopular in the seventeenth century.
   B. literature will endure long after all is destroyed in a culture.
   C. modern culture could be destroyed as it was during the Dark Ages.
   D. Both B and C are correct.

4. What does the phrase "profit by" mean in the context of this passage?
   A. learn from
   B. expand upon
   C. make money from
   D. lessen the importance of

Lesson Ten

1. **fallible** (făl´ ə bəl) *adj.* capable of error
Because we are all human, we all make mistakes; therefore, we are all *fallible.*
syn: imperfect *ant:* infallible, unerring

2. **fallow** (făl´ ō) *adj.* inactive; unproductive
A *fallow* mind needs to be stimulated.
syn: dormant, idle *ant:* fertile, productive

3. **farcical** (fär´ si kəl) *adj.* absurd; ridiculously clumsy
If three people had not been seriously injured, the botched bank robbery would have been *farcical.*
syn: ludicrous, funny *ant:* somber, serious

4. **fatalistic** (fāt əl ĭs´ tĭk) *adj.* believing that all things in life are inevitable, determined by fate
My father used to say that if you have a *fatalistic* attitude about life, you are most likely to think there is nothing you can do to change the course of it.

5. **fawn** (fôn) *verb* to act slavishly submissive
The young dancers *fawned* over the prima ballerina.
syn: kowtow, grovel

6. **fealty** (fē´ əl tē) loyalty; faithfulness
Because serfs owed *fealty* to their lords, disloyalty was punishable by death.
syn: devotion, fidelity, allegiance *ant:* disloyalty

7. **feign** (fān) *verb* to pretend
He *feigned* an interest in the conversation, but his mind wandered elsewhere.
syn: simulate, fake

8. **feisty** (fī´ stē) *adj.* aggressive; lively, energetic
Because the tiger cub was small but *feisty*, we approached him warily.
syn: quarrelsome, exuberant, spunky

9. **felicity** (fə lĭs´ ĭ tē) *noun* happiness
A contented person, rich or poor, is more likely to enjoy *felicity* than a discontented one.
ant: unhappiness, discontent

10. **felonious** (fə lō´ nē əs) *adj.* of, like, or constituting a felony (major crime)
The boys were charged with *felonious* assault and spent the night behind bars.

11. **fester** (fĕs´ tər) *verb* to rot; to form pus; to grow embittered
If allowed to *fester*, a feeling of dislike can turn to hatred.
syn: rankle

12. **fiat** (fī´ ăt) *noun* an official order
After seizing power, the general ruled by *fiat* backed by guns.
syn: decree, authorization

13. **fidelity** (fĭ dĕl´ ĭ tē) *noun* faithfulness
The king told his people that their *fidelity* would be rewarded.
syn: loyalty, allegiance *ant:* treachery, disloyalty

14. **filch** (fĭlch) *verb* to steal
The woman *filched* my purse when I left the room to answer the telephone.
syn: pilfer, rob

15. **filial** (fĭl´ ē əl) *adj.* relating to a son or daughter
The love we have for our parents is termed *filial* love.
syn: dutiful

Exercise I Words in Context

Fill in the blanks with the correct vocabulary words needed to complete the sentences.

fiats **fidelity** **infallible** **fealty** **farcical** **feigned**

A. The king believed he was _______________ and demanded complete _______________ from his court. All _______________ issued from the throne were to be followed to the letter, no matter how _______________ they seemed to be.

B. Like the others, the Black Knight pledged his _______________ to the new king; but it was with a heavy heart, for he thought that the Norman King only _______________ an interest in the people of England.

felicity **felonious** **fallow** **filial** **feisty** **fawn**

C. He was a _______________ young man who questioned everything he was told. So it was a real surprise when he began to _______________ over the new female supervisor.

D. The reign of King Alfred was marked by fruitful harvests and great _______________. Lands that had long been _______________ now produced abundant crops. _______________ attacks by armed highwaymen ended, and children once again extended respect and _______________ love to their parents.

fatalistic **fester** **filched**

E. Although he never _______________ a penny in his life, the accusations of theft did not disturb him. He was a _______________ man who took whatever life handed him. He felt that if he allowed any resentment to creep into his life, it would begin to _______________ and eventually destroy him.

Exercise II Roots, Prefixes, and Suffixes

Study the entries and answer the questions that follow.

The root *ped/pod* refers to "foot."
The root *scop* means "watch."
The root *phob* means "fear."
The root *port* means "to carry, bring."

1. A creature with two legs is called a _______________, but a stand with three legs is called a _______________ .

2. If you had a fear of feet, you might be said to have a _______________ia; and if you have a fear of enclosed places, you are suffering from_______________ia, while a *bibliophobe* would fear _______________.

3. Give a literal meaning for these words.
   report import
   transport porter
   portable

4. You would use a *telescope* to see _______________, and you would use a *microscope* to view _______________. But if you want to know the *scope* of something, you want to see _______________.

Exercise III Usage Inferences

Choose the answer that best fits the situation.

1. A person most likely to engage in *fawning* would be
   A. the owner of a company.
   B. an accountant.
   C. a fan of a popular musician.
   D. a movie star.

2. A *feisty* person would probably not make a good
   A. policeman.
   B. diplomat.
   C. general.
   D. scientist.

3. *Filial* respect refers to the respect we show
   A. to our brothers and sisters.
   B. to our parents.
   C. to reverent and holy people.
   D. to elderly people.

Exercise IV Reading Comprehension

Read the selection and answer the questions.

Gordon Berry says there should be more to children's television than cuddly bears. "We should force children to reach for ideas as we entertain them," said Berry, an educational psychologist who spends a lot of time looking at children's shows and considering their effect on youngsters.

"They need shows with hard-hitting content as well as cuddly bears. Children are not little adults, but we do need to challenge them more. We should challenge them with a range of offerings, and I don't mean to exclude animation because it can also be challenging," Berry said.

He is a professor in the Graduate School of Education at UCLA, where he teaches courses in educational psychology and a course on "Children and Television" in the communications studies area.

"I don't think we have enough diversity in the types of programs that are available," he said. "Children, like adults, need a range of program offerings. They need live-action shows as well as animation."

1. With which statement would Gordon Berry most likely disagree?
   A. Watching too much television can harm a child's intellectual development.
   B. Children would gain knowledge if there were more animation on television.
   C. More variety is needed in the television programs children are exposed to.
   D. Childhood education can be improved by providing better television programs.

2. The author states or implies that
   A. television is a wasteland as far as intellect is concerned.
   B. young children watch too much television.
   C. television doesn't challenge the minds of children enough.
   D. cartoon shows have little value.

3. From this article we might legitimately infer that Berry would also believe that
   A. parents don't spend enough time with their children.
   B. parents should read books to young children.
   C. children should attend pre-school to begin the learning process early.
   D. children should be given more responsibility for what they watch.

4. The main problem that Berry sees with children's television is that
   A. it contains too much violence.
   B. the animated cartoons are completely unbelievable.
   C. too many of the shows for children are the same.
   D. children spend too much time watching television.

Lesson Eleven

1. **flagrant** (flā´ grənt) *adj.* glaringly bad; outrageous
His *flagrant* disregard for authority got the boy into a lot of trouble.
syn: offensive

2. **fluent** (flōō´ ənt) *adj.* able to speak and/or write easily, clearly
Being *fluent* in three languages helped Ellen obtain the job of interpreter at the United Nations.
syn: flowing

3. **flux** (flŭks) *noun* a state of continual change or movement
The fashion industry is always in a state of *flux.*
syn: flow *ant:* inactivity

4. **foible** (foi´ bəl) *noun* a minor weakness in character
The cook's only *foible* was that she could not keep a secret and loved to gossip.
syn: weakness, fault

5. **fracas** (frā´ kəs) *noun* a loud quarrel
The coaches of the two teams broke up the *fracas* that began on the playing field after the game.
syn: brawl

6. **frivolous** (frĭv´ ə ləs) *adj.* trivial; silly
They argued over a *frivolous* point and wasted valuable time.
syn: foolish, trifling *ant:* vital, important

7. **futile** (fyōōt´ əl) *adj.* useless
My *futile* attempts to repair the broken vase left me frustrated.
syn: ineffectual, fruitless *ant:* successful, effective, profitable

8. **gaff** (găf) *noun* a large hook
A large side of beef swung from a *gaff* in the butcher shop.

9. **gait** (gāt) *noun* the manner of walking
The horse's smooth *gait* made riding him seem almost effortless.

10. **gambit** (găm´ bĭt) *noun* an opening maneuver or action one uses to gain advantage
I was wise to his *gambit,* so I did not take the easy jump he gave me.
syn: strategy

11. **gape** (gāp) *verb* to stare with an open mouth
The child *gaped* at his mother in astonishment.

12. **garble** (gär´ bəl) *verb* to distort or confuse either intentionally or unintentionally
The boy tried not to, but he *garbled* the message because of his sore tongue.
syn: mix up, mislead

13. **genealogy** (jē´ nē ăl´ ə jē) *noun* family history; the study of ancestry
His *genealogy* was recorded in the family Bible.
syn: lineage

14. **genesis** (jĕn´ ə sĭs) *noun* the beginning; origin
The professor said each civilization creates its own myth to explain its *genesis*.
syn: creation

15. **ghastly** (găst´ lē) *adj.* horrible; frightful, ghost-like
There was a *ghastly* smile on the dead man's face; it was as if he had had the last laugh.
syn: dreadful, hideous *ant:* lovely, attractive

Exercise I Words in Context

Fill in the blanks with the correct vocabulary words needed to complete the sentences.

foible **fluent** **gaff** **futile** **flagrant**

A. Although he considered his habit of telling white lies a mere ________________ , others said of him that he had a ________________ disregard for the truth.

B. Kris had taken French in high school, but she was not ________________ in the language. When she visited Paris, she realized it was ________________ to try to hold a conversation with anyone, so her friend acted as her translator.

C. Most of the fish Will caught were easy to reel in, but when he caught a large tuna, he needed to use a ________________ to get it out of the water.

ghastly **genesis** **genealogy** **gape**

D. It was such a ________________ thing for Sally to say that Jim could only stand there and ________________ at her.

E. In researching her ________________, Abbey was able to trace the ________________ of her family back hundreds of years to its beginning in Scotland.

garble **flux** **fracas** **frivolous** **gait** **gambit**

F. It was a ________________ that the con man often used. With a limping ________________, he approached someone leaving a bank. He started an argument over something ________________. During the ________________, his accomplice came over and stole the victim's wallet while pretending to help him.

G. "I did not ________________ the message," I replied angrily. "The general said that the mission is canceled because the situation is in a state of ________________."

Exercise II Roots, Prefixes, and Suffixes

Study the entries and answer the questions that follow.

The root *scrib/script* means "to write."
The root *tempor* means "time."
The root *stru/struct* means "to build."
The root *therm* means "heat."

A. A *thermometer* measures _______________, but if we want to keep something hot or something cold, we would put either of them in a _______________. The word which means "pertaining to heat" is _______________ al.

B. List as many words as you can think of that contain the roots *stru/struct*.

C. The word *temporal* means _______________; if someone were asked to stand and give a speech right at this time, it is said that he is speaking _______________ously. The phrase "to temporize" means that one must suit his or her actions to the _______________.

D. A *conscript* is one whose name is _______________. While a *prescription* is a _______________, a *description* is a _______________.

Exercise III Usage Inferences

Choose the answer that best fits the situation.

1. Which of the following is the best example of an action that would be described as *flagrant*?
   A. soldiers capturing an enemy troop
   B. being five minutes late for curfew
   C. a robber holding up a bank at noon
   D. using incorrect grammar on an essay

2. The *genesis* of an invention is the
   A. initial idea of it.
   B. finished product.
   C. money invested in it.
   D. sales it generates.

3. If you are involved in a *futile* project, you will most likely feel
   A. confused.
   B. frustrated.
   C. intelligent.
   D. successful.

Exercise IV Reading Comprehension

Read the selection and answer the questions.

To a coalition of farmers, religious leaders, and animal welfare groups, it amounts to "patenting life" and will endanger humanity's relation to the natural world.

To business executives and ethicists, there is little difference between the breeding of a racehorse—a genetic manipulation carried out by traditional selection methods—and the raising of a leaner pig using the laboratory manipulation of genes known as "genetic engineering." Not surprisingly, the rhetoric generated by the Patent and Trademark Office's decision that *genetically altered animals are patentable* has been intense because the debate quickly shifts to a larger question—whether humans should use these powerful techniques to manipulate genes, the stuff of life.

The patent office touched off the debate when it reversed a long-standing position that living matter cannot be patented and extended patent ability to all creatures from cockroaches to cows, excepting only humans.

A typical "patentable animal" mentioned is a pig that might have a growth-promoting gene from a human inserted into its cells, making the animal grow meatier faster. The result might be leaner pork. Another example is the effort to put extra genes into the mammary tissue of animals so they would manufacture more nutritious milk.

1. What is the author's main point?
   A. to ridicule the patenting of living things
   B. to praise the patenting of living things
   C. to report on the patenting of living things
   D. to explain how to patent living things

2. The writer appears to be
   A. for the patenting of animals.
   B. against the patenting of animals.
   C. neither for or against the patenting of animals.
   D. of the opinion that the whole argument is ridiculous.

3. The best title for this selection is
   A. End Patents on Animal Life.
   B. Patenting Life—The Argument Resumes.
   C. Genetic Engineering—A Boon to Mankind.
   D. Leaner Pigs and Faster Horses.

4. The author also states or implies that
   A. businessmen who invest in creating better milk cows should be encouraged.
   B. some people believe it is wrong to manipulate the genes of any living creature.
   C. a leaner pig or better milk cow could be very beneficial to the world's poor.
   D. the patent office doesn't know what it wants to do.

Lesson Twelve

1. **gird** (gûrd) *verb* to encircle with a belt or band; to prepare for action; to equip
Before mounting his horse, the knight *girded* himself in armor.
syn: enclose, surround

2. **gist** (jĭst) *noun* the main point
I never did get the *gist* of his story.
syn: essence

3. **glean** (glēn) *verb* to collect or find out slowly, in small pieces; to gather (grain)
The investigator *gleaned* pertinent information from the witnesses to the crash.
syn: ascertain

4. **glutinous** (glōōt´ n əs) *adj.* gluey, sticky
The *glutinous* mass I was kneading on the counter in no way resembled the bread dough pictured in the cookbook.

5. **gorge** (gôrj) *verb* to eat or swallow greedily
The starving youngster began to *gorge* himself with a plateful of sandwiches.

6. **Gothic** (gŏth´ ĭk) *adj.* medieval; a genre of literature that includes romantic and supernatural elements
The Warlock is a *Gothic* novel with a little romance thrown in to lighten the mood.

7. **granary** (grān´ ə rē) *noun* a storehouse for grain
When the *granary* burned down, we lost a year's supply of corn.

8. **gratify** (grăt´ ə fī) *verb* to please
To *gratify* the pouting child, his mother handed him a lollipop.
syn: satisfy, indulge *ant:* displease, dissatisfy

9. **guile** (gīl) *noun* slyness and cunning in dealing with others
Not without *guile* herself, she was quick to recognize it in others.
syn: cunning, craftiness *ant:* ingenuousness

10. **gull** (gŭl) *verb* to cheat
An honest car salesman would not *gull* his customers.
syn: trick

11. **gyrate** (jī´ rāt) *verb* to rotate, spin
The kite began to *gyrate* crazily as the winds picked up speed.
syn: revolve, whirl

12. **harp** (härp) *verb* to persist in talking continuously (on or about something)
My parents *harp* on the importance of completing homework.

13. **haughty** (hô´ tē) *adj.* arrogant, proud
He gave them a *haughty* look as he waved the visitors through the gates.
syn: disdainful, lofty *ant:* humble, shy

14. **havoc** (hăv´ ək) *noun* great destruction
The commandos landed behind enemy lines in order to create confusion and *havoc.*

15. **hilarity** (hĭ lăr´ ĭ tē) *noun* gaiety, joy
Because of the *hilarity* at my slumber party, everyone was awake all night.
syn: mirth *ant:* sadness, misery

Exercise I Words in Context

Fill in the blanks with the correct vocabulary words needed to complete the sentences.

gird **havoc** **gorged** **glutinous**

A. The _______________ rice was hard to eat, but I _______________ myself on it anyway because I was really hungry.

B. Alicia had to _______________ herself for babysitting the twins who had a reputation for creating _______________ when their parents were away.

glean **granary** **guile** **harped** **hilarious**

C. In some communities, farmers allow charitable organizations to _______________ the fields after the harvest. Whatever they collect is stored in a _______________ to be made into bread and other food for the poor.

D. The kids thought it was _______________ when Mike did a belly flop into the pool. When he got out of the water, his parents _______________ on him about how he could have gotten hurt by being reckless. However, Mike used _______________ to convince them that he had been pushed off the diving board, but didn't see who did it.

gist **gull** **Gothic** **haughty** **gratified** **gyrated**

E. Because Sally was trying to pick up the _______________ of the conversation at the next table, she did not see the waiter standing at her side. Finally, in a _______________ manner, the waiter said, "Whenever you are ready to stop snooping and order, please let me know."

F. It is a typical _______________ novel, with a swooning heroine and a dark, good-looking hero. The villain, of course, is the hero's stepbrother, who is trying to _______________ the heroine out of her considerable fortune.

G. When my parents were children, they played with spinning tops, which _______________ when they they were twirled. They said getting the tops to spin longer than anyone else's _______________ them and made for some fun competitions.

Exercise II Roots, Prefixes, and Suffixes

Study the entries and answer the questions that follow.

The root *tract* means "to man." The root *anthro* means "man."

The root *ven/vent* means "to come." The suffix *–ology* means "the study of."

A. The study of man must be _______________, but one who hates mankind is a mis_______________. A creature that resembles man is called an _______________oid.

B. List other words you can think of that end in *–ology* and, as well as you can, identify what the word is a study of.

C. Give the literal meaning of these words:
convention
prevention
invention

D. If you draw something away from someone's reputation, _______________ from it, but if you draw someone's attention away, you _______________ them. To draw away a small portion from a larger whole is to _______________, but a noun meaning something that draws people together is _______________.

Exercise III Usage Inferences

Choose the answer that best fits the situation.

1. An air of *hilarity* is most likely to be found
   A. in a classroom.
   B. in a church.
   C. at a shopping mall.
   D. at a comedy club.

2. If you touch a *glutinous* substance, it will
   A. dissolve.
   B. change color.
   C. feel sticky.
   D. burn you.

3. It takes *guile* to
   A. play a prank on someone.
   B. give a speech in class.
   C. stay up to see the sun rise.
   D. plan a low-budget vacation.

Exercise IV Reading Comprehension

Read the selection and answer the questions.

A new book warning that a decline in the birth rate in the industrial world will be accompanied by a decrease in the global influence of Western democratic culture has provoked heated criticism, especially from groups advocating population control.

The book, *The Birth Dearth*, is written by Ben J. Wattenberg, a Democrat frequently critical of his party for being too liberal. He is the author of a number of books on political, economic, and cultural trends. The book warns that declining fertility in the developed nations while population growth rates are soaring in the developing world will weaken the political, military, and cultural position of industrial countries because they will constitute a smaller fraction of the global population.

Mr. Wattenberg urges, therefore, that the United States and other industrial countries adopt policies to encourage couples to have children. These policies would include paid maternity leave, paid day care, and tax incentives.

Groups who advocate population control argue that a recommendation for higher birth rates is not needed. They point out that we live in a world expected to grow by still another billion people before babies now being born graduate from high school. Furthermore, some critics of Mr. Wattenberg's theories say they are tinged with racism.

1. Which statement most accurately summarizes one of Wattenburg's positions?
   A. A decreasing birth rate is a symptom of a racist world.
   B. Fewer births result in a stronger national economy.
   C. Fewer deaths in industrial countries make them stronger.
   D. Governmental policies should encourage higher birth rates.

2. As presented in this review, the major thesis of the book *The Birth Dearth* is that
   A. there must be more done to curb the population explosion in third world countries.
   B. a declining birth rate in developed nations will weaken their world position.
   C. limiting the number of children per family in the U.S. may become necessary in the future.
   D. Both A and C are correct.

3. The best title for this selection is
   A. The Birth Dearth—A Bust.
   B. New Book Arouses Controversy.
   C. No More Children—Says Wattenberg.
   D. Procreate or Vanish.

4. Mr. Wattenberg is suggesting that
   A. industrial nations should have more children.
   B. underdeveloped countries are increasing their population, while the population of developed countries is decreasing.
   C. the governments in industrial countries should provide incentives to have children.
   D. All of the above are correct.

Lesson Thirteen

1. **holocaust** (hŏl´ ə kôst) *noun* a great or complete destruction of life (especially by fire)
The peaceful village had been turned into a *holocaust* by the fire bombs.

2. **homily** (hŏm´ ə lē) *noun* a sermon
"Sir," I said, "I need food and clothes for these people, not a *homily* on patience."
syn: lecture

3. **hone** (hōn) *verb* to sharpen
Before he went on a mission, he always *honed* his knife to a razor sharpness.
ant: dull

4. **hovel** (hŏv´əl) *noun* a dirty, wretched living place; an open shed
The social worker looked with distaste at the dreary *hovel* in which the children were living.

5. **humane** (hyōō mān´) *adj.* kind; compassionate
The veterinarian told us that putting the injured horse to sleep was the only *humane* thing to do.
syn: tender, merciful, considerate *ant:* inhumane, cruel

6. **imbibe** (ĭm bīb´) *verb* to drink; to take in (ideas or knowledge)
During games, players must *imbibe* a great deal of water to stay hydrated.

7. **imbue** (ĭm byōō´) *verb* to fill completely
He was so *imbued* with his country's ideals that he would gladly risk his life for them.
syn: saturate, pervade

8. **immaculate** (im măk´ yə lĭt) *adj.* spotless; pure, flawless
The rooms were as *immaculate* as the grounds surrounding the large estate.
syn: clean, virtuous, errorless *ant:* dirty, corrupt, imperfect

9. **impede** (ĭm pēd´) *verb* to hinder, obstruct
The car broken down in the middle of the road *impeded* the flow of traffic.
syn: delay, retard *ant:* aid, encourage

10. **impel** (ĭm pĕl´) *verb* to push into motion
Impelled by hunger and thirst, the man staggered across the desert.
syn: urge, force, propel, drive *ant:* restrain

11. **impermeable** (ĭm pûr´ mē ə bəl) *adj.* not permitting passage (especially of fluids)
Because the map case was made of rubber, it was *impermeable* to water.
syn: impenetrable *ant:* permeable

12. **impertinent** (ĭm pûr´ tn ənt) *adj.* rude and disrespectful
The boy was suspended from school for his *impertinent* behavior.
syn: impudent, insolent *ant:* polite, courteous

13. **imperturbable** (ĭm pər tûr´ bə bəl) *adj.* not easily excited or upset, even under pressure
The captain's *imperturbable* manner had a quieting effect on his men.
syn: cool, steady, calm *ant:* excitable

14. **impervious** (ĭm pûr´ vē əs) *adj.* not capable of being affected by
The wounded man seemed *impervious* to pain as he continued to move toward his enemy.
syn: resistant *ant:* vulnerable

15. **impetuous** (ĭm pĕch´ o͞o əs) *adj.* acting suddenly without thought
Impetuous behavior can be hazardous to your health.
syn: impulsive *ant:* planned, careful

Exercise I Words in Context

Fill in the blanks with the correct vocabulary words needed to complete the sentences.

homilies **holocaust** **hovel** **imbibe** **immaculate** **humane**

A. Ellen's parents had taught her how to properly care for a home, so when she moved into her first apartment, she was quickly able to transform it from a filthy ________________ to a(n) ________________ home.

B. After the ________________ destroyed an entire city block, over one hundred families were without a place to live. Unfortunately, although the politicians made speeches and the clergy gave ________________ about charity, only a few ________________ individuals helped the homeless people.

C. David's one unhealthy habit is his need to ________________ in great quantities of coffee in the morning to start his day.

impertinent **impetuous** **impervious** **impelled** **impeded**

D. The judge was _______________ to the defendant's tears and pleas for leniency. He explained that her _______________ decision to steal a car for fun was still a crime even though she returned the vehicle to the owner undamaged.

E. Kate tried to explain to her teacher that she had been _______________ to take some shortcuts on the project because her lab partner's sloppy mistakes had _______________ their progress. Kate's _______________ comment earned her a trip to the principal's office.

impermeable **imbue** **hone** **imperturbable**

F. My father always strived to _______________ me with a spirit of excellence. "If you are going to _______________ your skills," he always said, "you must practice, practice, practice."

G. Andrew was a(n) _______________ individual who would not let disaster upset his steady calmness. He had worked hard to repair his damaged boat with several coats of a new product that was supposed to be _______________ to water. When the sea started seeping through the hull on his first trip out, Andrew grinned and said, "Oh well, it was worth a try."

Exercise II Roots, Prefixes, and Suffixes

Study the entries and answer the questions that follow.

The root *am* means "friend," "love."
The root *brev* means "short."
The root *aqu* means "water."

A. Something that is shortened, the name of a state for example, is an _______________. A story that is noted for its *brevity* is a _______________.

B. Someone who is friendly is said to be _______________iable or _______________cable. If you are in a loving mood, you might be called _______________orous; but if you feel only friendship for someone, you are said to have _______________ity.

C. List as many words as you can think of with the root *aqu* in them.

Exercise III Usage Inferences

Choose the answer that best fits the situation.

1. In what career is it necessary to be *imperturbable*?
   A. an actor
   B. an accountant
   C. a paramedic
   D. a mechanic

2. Which would you most likely *hone*?
   A. rough skin
   B. your study skills
   C. a new car
   D. the kitchen floor

3. Which of the following would most likely *impede* the progress of a road construction project?
   A. heavy traffic
   B. extra workers
   C. new equipment
   D. bad weather

Exercise IV Reading Comprehension

Read the selection and answer the questions.

I have often thought of it as one of the most barbarous customs in the world, that we deny the advantages of learning to women. We reproach the sex every day with folly and impertinence, while I am confident, had they the advantages of education equal to us, they would be guilty of less than ourselves.

One would wonder, indeed how it should happen that women are conversable at all. Their youth is spent to teach them to stitch and sew or make baubles. They are taught to read, indeed, and perhaps to write their names or so, and that is the height of a woman's education. And I would but ask any who slight the sex for their understanding, what is a man (a gentleman, I mean) good for that is taught no more?

The soul is placed in the body like a rough diamond, and must be polished, or the luster of it will never appear: and 'tis manifest that as the rational soul distinguishes us from brutes, so education carries on the distinction and makes some less brutish than others. This is too evident to need any demonstration. But why then should women be denied the benefit of instruction? If knowledge and understanding had been useless additions to the sex, God Almighty would never have given them capacities, for He made nothing needless. Besides, I would ask such what they can see in ignorance that they should think it a necessary ornament to a woman? Or how much worse is a wise woman than a fool? Or what has the woman done to forfeit the privilege of being taught? Does she plague us with her pride and impertinence? Why did we not let her learn, that she might have had more wit? Shall we upbraid women with folly, when 'tis only the error of this inhuman custom that hindered them being made wiser?

Daniel Defoe

1. What does the author say about the human soul?
   A. Everyone has a soul, even if he or she is unaware of it.
   B. The soul is not something that can be improved upon.
   C. Education is not something that can assist the growth of the soul.
   D. The human soul needs to be worked on, or it will disappear.

2. The author's primary purpose seems to be to
   A. encourage women to go to college.
   B. condemn men for the way they treat women.
   C. change the way men regard women and education.
   D. make excuses for women's lack of intellect.

3. The author's tone in this selection seems to be one of
   A. patient understanding.
   B. mild impatience.
   C. calm reflection.
   D. wild denunciation.

4. The author states or implies that
   A. far too many women have been denied an education by men.
   B. men have denied women an education because they fear them.
   C. it is simply a custom of the times that women are denied an education.
   D. Both A and C are correct.

Lesson Fourteen

1. **jaded** (jā´ dĭd) *adj.* worn out; dulled, as from overindulgence
After touring seemingly endless rooms of ancient paintings, the students were too *jaded* to look at the modern art exhibit.
syn: tired, wearied *ant:* fresh

2. **jargon** (jär´ gən) *noun* vocabulary specific to a particular group of people
Sara was amused by the band's *jargon* at first, but she eventually began to feel left out of their conversations.
syn: dialect, language

3. **judicious** (jōō dĭsh´ əs) *adj.* showing sound judgment
A *judicious* manager should treat everyone the same way and not show favoritism.
syn: wise, careful *ant:* unwise, impractical, unsound

4. **kindred** (kĭn´ drĭd) *adj.* related by birth; of like nature
The boy and his dog were *kindred* spirits who spent the day running and jumping in the woods.
syn: similar

5. **knead** (nēd) *verb* to work dough or clay into a uniform mixture
It is easier to *knead* bread dough with an electric mixer than by hand.
syn: squeeze, rub, press

6. **lacerate** (lăs´ ə rāt) *verb* to tear jaggedly
Harsh criticism can cut into one's pride just as easily as a sharp knife can *lacerate* the skin.
syn: mangle, maim

7. **lackadaisical** (lăk ə dā´ zĭ kəl) *adj.* uninterested, listless
The workers, usually *lackadaisical* by late afternoon, suddenly moved with great energy.
syn: spiritless, languid *ant:* enthusiastic, inspired

8. **lackey** (lăk´ ē) *noun* a slavish follower
I will not deal with a *lackey*; I'll talk to the boss or no one.

9. **laggard** (lăg´ ərd) *noun* someone or something that is slow to progress; one who lags behind
In the wild, some predators attack the weaklings and *laggards* of a group when hunting.
syn: loiterer

10. **lament** (lə mĕnt´) *verb* to mourn; to show sadness or regret
Thousands of devoted fans *lamented* the death of the popular singer.
syn: grieve *ant:* rejoice

11. **lampoon** (lăm po͞on´) *noun* a written satire used to ridicule or attack
The *lampoon* he wrote in the school newspaper angered the football coach and the principal.
syn: parody, caricature

12. **languish** (lăng´ gwĭsh) *verb* to become weak, feeble, or depressed; to be neglected or ignored
After the administrator was fired, scholarship applications *languished* on her desk until someone was hired to replace her.
syn: wither, fade *ant:* thrive

13. **lateral** (lăt´ ər əl) *adj.* to the side
The quarterback made a *lateral* pass to the fullback.
syn: sideways

14. **lax** (lăks) *adj.* careless or negligent
Don't become too *lax* in your studies, or you'll fail.
syn: slack, neglectful *ant:* careful, meticulous

15. **lethal** (lē´ thəl) *adj.* deadly, fatal
Because the fumes from the *lethal* gas were overpowering, many people collapsed.

Exercise I Words in Context

Fill in the blanks with the correct vocabulary words needed to complete the sentences.

lament **lethal** **judicious** **lacerate**

A. We can do more than just ______________ Charlie's passing. We can work to change the boxing rules. Charlie's manager was not ______________in choosing opponents for Charlie and put him in the ring with a fighter at a higher skill level. The man had a ______________ left hook that had injured several other inexperienced fighters, and his power punches could______________ a young fighter's face in minutes.

lackadaisical **lateral** **kindred** **lackey** **lax**

B. Darryl was a ______________ employee: He wasted a lot of time chatting with coworkers, often missed deadlines, and was always late for work. Unfortunately, his boss was ______________ in enforcing the rules. Darryl was never disciplined for his behavior. In fact, he and his boss shared so many of the same attributes that they seemed like ______________ spirits.

C. During the competition, Rob moved his piece forward and didn't see that Jake could make a ______________ move across the board and win the game. Afterwards, Jake shook Rob's hand, but Jake's ______________, who had fetched him water throughout the game, laughed and made a cruel remark about the mistake that had cost Rob the game.

jargon **languished** **kneaded** **jaded** **lampoon** **laggards**

D. The daily newspaper usually prints a ______________ of the latest political controversy. Sometimes, I'm unfamiliar with the ______________ used and, therefore, don't get the full meaning of the joke.

E. After years of teaching disinterested children, who never practiced, the ______________ piano teacher quit, saying that she just couldn't take the ______________ who were wasting her time and their parents' money anymore.

F. My first attempt at baking bread was a disaster. I put the ingredients into the bread maker and turned it on. When I went to check on it later, I found that I had attached the mixers wrong and the machine hadn't ______________ the dough. The ingredients had ______________ in the bread maker all day and were ruined.

Exercise II Roots, Prefixes, and Suffixes

Study the entries and answer the questions that follow.

The suffix *–ism* means "belief in" or "practice of."
The root *cent* refers to "one hundred."
The root *dec* refers to "ten."
The root *duc/duct* means "to lead."
The prefix *anti–* means "against."

A. An *antibiotic* is ______________, an *antidote* is ______________, and a type of soap that fights against germs is called ______________.

B. List as many words as you can think of that contain the root *cent*.

C. A ten-year period is called a ______________ , and a word that originally meant to kill every tenth person is ______________imate.

D. List as many words as you can think of that contain the root *duc/duct*.

Exercise III Usage Inferences

Choose the answer that best fits the situation.

1. If you *lacerated* something, what would you most likely use?
   A. a knife
   B. a club
   C. a chair
   D. a key

2. Who is most likely to *lampoon* something?
   A. a fisherman
   B. a comedian
   C. a butcher
   D. a plumber

3. Which kind of person is **least** likely to be *judicious*?
   A. an immaculate person
   B. a fluent person
   C. an impetuous person
   D. a humane person

Exercise IV Reading Comprehension

Read the selection and answer the questions.

It is improbable that there was ever such a thing as a common human language. We know nothing of the language of Paleolithic man, and we do not even know whether Paleolithic man talked freely. We do know, though, that Paleolithic man had a keen sense of form and attitude. Because of his drawings it has been suggested that he communicated his ideas very largely by gesture. Probably such words as the earlier men used were mainly cries of alarm, or passion, or names for concrete things, and in many cases they were probably imitative sounds made by or associated with the things named. Sir Arthur Evans has suggested that in America, sign language is common to all Indians in North America, whereas the languages are different.

The first languages were probably small collections of interjections and nouns. Probably the nouns were said in different intonations to convey different meanings. If Paleolithic man had a word for "horse" or "bear," he probably showed by tone or gesture whether he meant "bear is coming," "bear is going," "bear is to be hunted," "dead bear," "bear has been here," "bear did this," and so on.

Only very slowly did the human mind develop methods of indicating action and relationship in a formal manner. Modern languages contain many thousands of words, but the earlier languages could have consisted of only a few hundred. It is said that even modern European peasants can get along with something less than a thousand words, and it is quite conceivable that as late as the Early Neolithic Period, that was the limit of the available vocabulary. Probably men did not indulge in those days in conversation or description. For narrative purposes they danced and acted rather than told. Even their powers of counting seem to have been very limited.

The growth of speech was at first a very slow process indeed, and grammatical forms and the expression of abstract ideas may have come very late in human history, perhaps only 400 or 500 generations ago.

The students of languages (philologists) tell us that they are unable to trace with certainty any common features in all the languages of mankind. They find over great areas, groups of languages which have similar root words and similar ways of expressing the same idea, but then they find in other areas, languages which appear to be dissimilar down to their fundamental structure, which express action and relation by entirely dissimilar devices, and have an altogether different grammatical scheme.

H. G. Wells

1. What is the main point of the passage?
   A. Language did not appear until very recently.
   B. Once language started, it developed very rapidly.
   C. Language developed very slowly over the centuries.
   D. Language developed because of the dangers people faced.

2. The author states or implies that
   A. man was born with the innate talent to speak but somehow lost this talent.
   B. early man communicated more by gesture than by speech.
   C. today the speaking vocabulary of the average person has been expanded by exposure to the mass media.
   D. philologists can trace all languages to one common language.

3. The author speculates that the first languages were probably
   A. Hebrew and Arabic.
   B. a small collection of interjections and nouns.
   C. gestures.
   D. never written down.

4. Regarding language, the author does not conclude that
   A. language probably began in Mesopotamia.
   B. early man's vocabulary was extremely limited.
   C. language to express concepts developed very slowly.
   D. there probably was never any common language.

Lesson Fifteen

1. **licentious** (lī sĕn´ shəs) *adj.* morally unrestrained or indifferent to laws or rules
His refusal to change his *licentious* behavior was the reason he spent most of his life in prison.
syn: immoral, lewd *ant:* moral, lawful

2. **macabre** (mə kä´ brə) *adj.* horrible; grim; relating to death
Dr. Jekyll's clean-cut features faded and were replaced by the *macabre* face of the hideous Mr. Hyde.
syn: ghastly, sinister *ant:* beautiful, lovely

3. **mandarin** (măn´ də rĭn) *noun* an influential person
There were nine classes of *mandarins* in the Chinese Empire.

4. **martial** (mär´ shəl) *adj.* warlike; military
After being defeated, the small country was ruled by *martial* law for several months.

5. **melee** (mā´ lā´) *noun* a noisy, confused fight
By the time the police arrived, the *melee* was over.

6. **mendicant** (mĕn´ dĭ kənt) *noun* a beggar
Although he was a *mendicant,* he begged not for himself, but for the poor and hungry.

7. **mesmerize** (mĕz´ mə rīz) *verb* to hypnotize
The exquisite music and spinning dancers *mesmerized* the audience.

8. **minion** (mĭn´ yən) *noun* a fawning, servile follower
Although only a *minion* who usually ran errands, on occasion he filled in for the "great one."
syn: lackey *ant:* leader

9. **mitigate** (mĭt´ ĭ gāt) *verb* to make less severe; to become milder
The injuries suffered by two recruits did not serve to *mitigate* the rigors of our basic training.
syn: relieve *ant:* exacerbate, aggravate

10. **modicum** (mŏd´ ĭ kəm) *noun* a small amount
A *modicum* of relief from the heat came in the form of a sudden shower.
syn: bit *ant:* abundance

11. **nadir** (nā´ dēr) *noun* the lowest point
Because of the violence and inhumanity, many thought that civilization had reached its *nadir* during this period.
ant: zenith

12. **narcissistic** (när´ sĭ sis tĭc) *adj.* conceited; one having excessive self-love and self-absorption
The child star's *narcissistic* attitude kept her from having any friends.
syn: vain *ant:* humble, modest

13. **nefarious** (nə fār´ ē əs) *adj.* very wicked
One of the most *nefarious* characters of the Old West was Billy the Kid.
syn: villainous *ant:* good, honest

14. **nemesis** (nĕm´ ĭ sĭs) *noun* someone or something a person cannot conquer or achieve; a hated enemy
Do you know the name of Sherlock Holmes's *nemesis?*
syn: rival, opponent

15. **neophyte** (nē´ ə fīt) *noun* a beginner
Although only a *neophyte*, she outshone the more seasoned performers.
syn: novice, amateur *ant:* expert, veteran

Exercise I Words in Context

Fill in the blanks with the correct vocabulary words needed to complete the sentences.

mesmerized **melee** **minion** **mendicant**

A. The police arrived in the park while the _______________ was at its peak. They did not want to arrest the poorly dressed _______________, but it was obvious that he had started the fight.

B. The audience was _______________ by the magician's talent. He and his _______________, whom he had sawed in half, were now engaged in the finale, which was the disappearing act.

modicum **neophyte** **mitigate** **macabre** **narcissistic**

C. He knew that he had to do something to _______________ the bad grades he was going to get that semester. He would see if he could do extra credit work; maybe with that and a _______________ of luck he would be able to pull through.

D. Although Darryl was a _______________ , he had solved his first few cases easily. He was so _______________ that he claimed to be the city's best detective. He proved that he was no better than anyone else, though, when he ran from the sight of a _______________ murder scene.

nemesis **mandarin** **nadir** **martial** **licentious** **nefarious**

E. When he awoke that morning, he felt at the ______________ of his life. He had never, never felt worse. At that moment, he vowed to give up his ______________ life and devote himself to sobriety and hard work.

F. The ______________ clapped his hands, and three servants came running. "Go," he ordered them, "and seek out the fiercest warrior in our kingdom. Be sure that this warrior possesses extraordinary ______________ skills, for all our lives will depend on him. There is a ______________ plot afoot to seize my palace; I am certain that my ______________, the evil Professor Autonucci, is behind this scheme."

Exercise II Roots, Prefixes, and Suffixes

Study the entries and answer the questions that follow.

The root *fort* means "strong."
The root *graph* means "to write."
The root *gen* means "race," "kind," "birth."
The prefix *mono–* means "one."

A. The quality or state of having strength is ______________ itude. A foreign word meaning an area of strength is ______________e, while to make something stronger is to ______________it.

B. Give a definition for the following *gen* words :

genealogy regenerate generate degenerate
generic genesis genocide

C. List as many words as you can think of that have *graph* as a root.

D. Without using a dictionary, define the following words as well as you can:

monograph monologue monolithic monotheism

Exercise III Usage Inferences

Choose the answer that best fits the situation.

1. You are most likely to meet a *mendicant*
   A. in a school.
   B. in a church.
   C. on the street.
   D. in an office.

2. If you have reached your *nadir*, you are likely to be feeling
   A. happy.
   B. proud.
   C. angry.
   D. depressed.

3. If you received a *modicum* of recognition for a difficult job you performed for your club, you would likely feel
   A. happy.
   B. proud.
   C. angry.
   D. depressed.

Exercise IV Reading Comprehension

Read the selection and answer the questions.

The best books are not read even by those who are called good readers. What does our Concord culture amount to? There is in this town, with a very few exceptions, no taste for the best or for very good books even in English literature, whose words all can read and spell. Even the college bred and so-called liberally educated men here and elsewhere have really little or no acquaintance with the English classics; and as for the recorded wisdom of mankind, the ancient classics and Bibles, which are accessible to all who will know of them, there are the feeblest efforts anywhere made to become acquainted with them.

I know a wood chopper, of middle age, who takes a French paper, not for news as he says, for he is above that, but to "keep himself in practice," he being a Canadian by birth; and when I ask him what he considers the best thing he can do in this world, he says, beside this, to keep up and add to his English. This is about as much as the college bred generally do or aspire to do, and they take an English paper for the purpose. One who has just come from reading perhaps one of the best English books will find how many with whom he can converse about it? Or suppose he comes from reading a Greek or Latin classic in the original, whose praises are familiar even to the so-called illiterate; he will find nobody at all to speak to, but must keep silence about it. Indeed, there is hardly the professor in our colleges, who, if he has mastered the difficulties of the language, has proportionally mastered the difficulties of the wit and poetry of a Greek poet, and has any sympathy to impart to the alert and heroic reader; and as for the sacred Scriptures, or Bibles of mankind, who in this town can tell me even their titles? Most men do not know that any nation but the Hebrews have had a scripture. A man, any man, will go considerably out of his way to pick up a silver dollar; but here are golden words, which the wisest men of antiquity have uttered, and whose worth the wise of every succeeding age have assured us of; —and yet we learn to read only as far as Easy Reading, the primers and class books, and when we leave school, the *Little Reading*, and story-books, which are for boys and beginners; and our reading, our conversation and thinking, are all on a very low level, worthy only of pygmies and mannequins.

I aspire to be acquainted with wiser men than this our Concord soil has produced, whose names are hardly known here. Or shall I hear the name of Plato and never read his book? As if Plato were my townsman and I never saw him, my next neighbor and I never heard him speak or attended to the wisdom of his words. But how actually is it? His *Dialogues*, which contain what was immortal in him, lie on the next shelf, and yet I never read them. We are underbred and low-lived and illiterate; and in this respect I confess I do not make any very broad distinction between the illiterateness of my townsman who cannot read at all and the illiterateness of him who has learned to read only what is for children and feeble intellects. We should be as good as the worthies of antiquity, but partly by first knowing how good they were. We are a race of little men, and soar but little higher in our intellectual flights than the columns of the daily paper.

Henry David Thoreau

1. With which statement would the author most likely agree?
   A. Most people read as much as they should, despite being busy.
   B. More people should read the Bible than those who currently do.
   C. Most people who read a great book will discuss it with others.
   D. People will be improved even by reading things like newspapers.

2. The author states or implies that
   A. the rate of illiteracy in Concord is very high because there are no schools.
   B. very few people in Concord have read any of the classics in their original language.
   C. even those who can read do not read anything but the newspaper.
   D. Both B and C are correct.

3. The tone of this selection is best described as
   A. quiet reflection.
   B. angry denunciation.
   C. impatient annoyance.
   D. gleeful gloating.

4. This selection especially criticizes
   A. those who can read the classics but don't.
   B. schools that failed to teach the populace to read.
   C. people who never bothered to learn how to read.
   D. professors who teach classics at the colleges.

Lesson Sixteen

1. **nepotism** (nĕp´ ə tĭz əm) *noun* favoritism shown to a relative in business or politics, especially regarding hiring
Not wanting to be accused of *nepotism*, my Uncle Matthew refused to hire me even though I was qualified for the job.

2. **numismatist** (nōō mĭs´ mə tĭst) *noun* a coin collector
My father used to be an avid *numismatist* when he was a merchant and had access to a lot of small change.

3. **obeisance** (ō bā´ səns) *noun* a bow or similar gesture expressing deep respect
The crowd made *obeisances* as the king's carriage rolled past.

4. **obsequy** (ŏb´ sə kwē) *noun* a funeral rite or ceremony
At the graveside, a minister performed the *obsequies* before the body was lowered into the grave.

5. **obtrude** (əb trōōd´) *verb* to force oneself upon others unasked or unwanted; to push out
You were sitting there looking very thoughtful, and I did not wish to *obtrude*.
syn: intrude

6. **ogre** (ō´ gər) *noun* a monster; hideous being
When I was little, the *ogre* in that movie scared me; now that I'm older, it looks pretty silly.

7. **opiate** (ō´ pē ĭt) *noun* a narcotic; anything causing sleep or bringing relief
A mild *opiate* was used to quiet the wounded animal.
ant: stimulant

8. **oscillate** (ŏs´ ə lāt) *verb* to swing or move back and forth like a pendulum.
I felt my loyalty *oscillate* between the candidates as each one said certain things with which I agreed.
syn: vacillate, fluctuate, vary

9. **ostentatious** (ŏs tĕn tā´ shəs) *adj.* marked by a conspicuous, showy, or pretentious display
It was an *ostentatious* affair, meant to impress the hundreds of wealthy guests.

10. **oust** (oust) *verb* to drive out; expel; dispossess
The bailiff began to *oust* the disruptive spectators from the courtroom.

11. **pacify** (păs´ ə fī) *verb* to calm down
No one was able to *pacify* the crying baby except her grandmother.
syn: appease, placate *ant:* incite, agitate

12. **paean** (pē´ ăn) *noun* a song of praise or joy
The ceremony was marked by colorful rituals and beautiful *paeans* sung by a monk's choir.

13. **pall** (pôl) *noun* something that covers or conceals
A *pall* of gloom descended over the crowd.

14. **pallid** (păl´ ĭd) *adj.* pale; faint in color
The patient's *pallid* face and slow, raspy breathing concerned the doctor.
ant: hearty, robust

15. **palpable** (păl´ pə bəl) *adj.* obvious; capable of being touched or felt
The fear in the room was so *palpable* that Krietzer thought it could be cut with a knife.
syn: evident, tangible *ant:* obscure, unclear

Exercise I Words in Context

Fill in the blanks with the correct vocabulary words needed to complete the sentences.

nepotism **opiate** **pacify** **ogre**

A. In order to ________________ the reporter, the president of the company finally granted him an interview. But when the reporter accused him of ________________ because of the five family members he had hired, the reporter was thrown out of the president's office.

B. For some people, the________________ made them sleepy; however, when Bart took it, he turned into an ________________ who fought and argued with everyone.

obsequy **pall** **oust** **obeisance** **palpable**

C. In a gesture of ___________ people lined the streets and bowed their heads during the popular former president's funeral procession. At the graveside, he received a twenty-one gun salute after the minister read the ________________.

D. A________________ of gloom settled over the senator's campaign headquarters. The candidate who wanted to________________ the senator from office was gaining the lead in the polls. As is became clear that the senator would not be re-elected, the tension in the room was so ________________ that you could feel it.

obtruded **pallid** **numismatist** **oscillated** **paean** **ostentatious**

E. It was hard to like her. She_______________ her opinion into other people's conversations without reservation. In addition, she loved to show off her wealth. The _______________ way she dressed and decorated her house made it clear that all she cared about was money.

F. The shop owner stepped out of the back room to show us his collection. From his _______________ complexion, it was clear he didn't often leave his office to get some fresh air and sunshine. The _______________ was certainly dedicated to his passion for rare coins.

G. As he walked down the aisle, the priest _______________ the container of incense and sang a traditional _______________.

Exercise II Roots, Prefixes, and Suffixes

Study the entries and answer the questions that follow.

The prefix *ambi/amphi–* means "both."
The root *luc/lum* means "light."
The prefix *super–* means "above, beyond."
The root *magn* means "great."

A. If someone watching you play ball says that you are *ambidextrous*, he means that you can _______________. If he says that you have *ambivalent* feelings about a friend, he probably means that you _______________ that person. If someone makes an *ambiguous* comment, it could be taken in _______________. A creature that is *amphibious* could live _______________.

B. List as many words as you can think of that contain the prefix *super–*.

C. If you *illuminate* a room, you _______________; if you *elucidate* on a comment, you _______________. So, something that is *lucid* is _______________, and something in the heavens that is *luminous* is _______________.

D. Define the italicized word.
a *magnanimous* person
a *magnate* in the auto industry
the *magnitude* of the disaster
the *magnificent* spectacle

Exercise III Usage Inferences

Choose the answer that best fits the situation.

1. Which of the following could be considered *obtrusive*?
   A. voicing an uninvited opinion
   B. sending a sympathy card
   C. stealing someone's parking spot
   D. eating the last piece of cake

2. Which of the following doesn't need to be *pacified*?
   A. a pet
   B. a child
   C. a soldier
   D. a craving

3. *Ostentatiousness* is most likely to be found
   A. at a dinner party.
   B. at a skating rink.
   C. in a school.
   D. in a courtroom.

Exercise IV Reading Comprehension

Read the selection and answer the questions.

After the [Japanese] conquer us and put us to the sword, and the republic descends into hell, some literary don of Oxford will surely notice, in reviewing our literary history, the curious persistence with which the literary critics native to the land have overlooked its emerging men of letters. I mean, of course, its genuine men of letters, its salient and truly original men, its men of intrinsic and unmistakable distinction. The fourth-raters have fared well enough, God knows. Go back to any standard literature book of ten, or twenty, or thirty, or fifty years ago, and you will be amazed by its praise of shoddy mediocrities, long since fly-blown and forgotten. George William Curtis, now seldom heard of at all, save perhaps in the reminiscences of senile publishers, was treated in his day with all the deference due to a prince of the blood. Artemus Ward, Petroleum, V. Nasby and half a dozen other such hollow buffoons were ranked with Mark Twain, and even above him while Frank R. Stockton, for thirty years, was the delight of all right-thinking reviewers.

Meanwhile, three of the five indubitably first-rate artists that America has produced went quite without orthodox recognition at home until either foreign enthusiasm or domestic clamor from below forced them into a belated and grudging sort of notice. I need not say that I allude to Poe, Whitman and Mark Twain. If it ever occurred to any American critic of position, during Poe's lifetime, that he was a greater man than either Cooper or Irving, then I have been unable to find any trace of the fact in the critical literature of the time. The truth is that he was looked upon as a facile and somewhat dubious journalist, too cocksure by half, and not a man to be encouraged. Lowell praised him in 1845 and at the same time denounced the current over-praise of lesser men, but later on this encomium was diluted with very important reservations, and there the matter stood until Baudelaire discovered the poet and his belated fame came winging home. Whitman, as every one knows, fared even worse. Emerson first hailed him and then turned tail upon him, eager to avoid any share in his ill-repute among blockheads. No other critic of any influence gave him help. He was carried through his dark days of poverty and persecution by a few private enthusiasts, none of them with the ear of the public, and in the end it was Frenchmen and Englishmen who lifted him into the light. Imagine a Harvard Professor lecturing upon him in 1865! As for Mark Twain, the story of his first fifteen years has been admirably told by Prof. Dr. William Lyon Phelps, of Yale. The dons were unanimously against him. Some sneered at him as a feeble mountebank; others refused to discuss him at all; not one harbored the slightest suspicion that he was a man of genius, or even one leg of a man of genius.

H. L. Menken

1. What does the author say about Mark Twain?
   A. Twain was underrated as an author for many years.
   B. Twain does not deserve to be called a genius.
   C. Twain should be admired for his journalism.
   D. Twain is as great an author as Cooper or Irving.

2. The author states or implies that
   A. the critics praised fourth-rate writers and ignored the first-rate writers.
   B. Irving was a better writer than Cooper.
   C. Mark Twain was an overrated writer and not as good as Poe or Whitman.
   D. All of the above are correct.

3. Of Cooper and Irving, Menken seems to say that
   A. they are fourth-rate writers.
   B. they are first-rate writers who have been overlooked.
   C. they are among the first-rate but have not been overlooked.
   D. they are the two best of all the first-rate writers.

4. Among the fourth-rate writers, Menken includes
   A. Twain.
   B. Stockton.
   C. Poe.
   D. Whitman.

Lesson Seventeen

1. **pariah** (pə rī´ ə) *noun* an outcast
He knew that he would become a *pariah* if he informed the authorities.

2. **patrician** (pə trĭsh´ ən) *noun* an aristocrat
Since he was a *patrician,* he couldn't marry the girl he loved because she was from a lower class.

3. **paucity** (pô´ sĭ tē) *noun* scarcity, a lack of something
Because of a *paucity* of imagination, he was not able to see beyond his immediate self-interest.
syn: insufficiency *ant:* abundance

4. **pedagogue** (pĕd´ ə gŏg) *noun* a schoolteacher
As an experienced *pedagogue*, Doug was a great asset to the school's English department.

5. **penchant** (pĕn´ chənt) *noun* a strong liking for
He had a *penchant* for small dogs with sharp, little barks.
syn: fondness, inclination, taste *ant:* dislike, abhorrence

6. **pensive** (pĕn´ sĭv) *adj.* dreamily thoughtful
A *pensive* mood came over the girl as she watched the sad movie.
syn: reflective, meditative *ant:* silly, frivolous

7. **penury** (pĕn´ yə rē) *noun* extreme poverty
Although born into *penury,* he became one of the country's richest men.
syn: destitution *ant:* wealth, opulence

8. **personification** (pĕr sŏn ə fĭ kā´ shən) *noun* a perfect example; a figure of speech in which a thing, quality, or idea is represented as a person
The old woman was the very *personification* of all things evil and cruel.

9. **quaff** (kwŏf) *verb* to drink in large quantities; to gulp
As soon as his shift was over, the thirsty hockey player *quaffed* water from a bottle the trainer gave him.

10. **qualm** (kwäm) *noun* a feeling of uneasiness
The boy had no *qualms* about cheating on the test.
syn: misgiving *ant:* ease, content, security

11. **query** (kwēr´ ē) *noun* a question
When I could not answer his *query,* he became very hostile.

12. **queue** (kyōō) *noun* a line of people waiting their turn
During the war, there were often long *queues* in front of the butcher shops because meat was in short supply.

13. **rabid** (răb´ ĭd) *adj.* intense; violent or raging; affected with rabies
Cortezzo was a *rabid* nationalist who would stop at nothing to further his cause.
syn: fanatical

14. **rambunctious** (răm bŭngk´ shəs) *adj.* unruly; uncontrollable exuberance
The *rambunctious* twins kept the house in an uproar from morning until night.
syn: wild, disorderly, boisterous *ant:* calm, pacific, tranquil

15. **rancid** (răn´ sĭd) *adj.* having a bad taste or smell; spoiled
The *rancid* meat gave a few people food poisoning.
syn: stale, repulsive *ant:* fresh

Exercise I Words in Context

Fill in the blanks with the correct vocabulary words needed to complete the sentences.

penchant **queues** **rambunctious** **pedagogue** **pariah**

1. As a ______________, professor Mullin had no equal, but she had never been nominated for teacher of the year. Nevertheless, students would stand in ______________ for hours in order to sign up for her classes.

2. The young, ______________ child could not be controlled. She became a ______________ at her pre-school because none of the other children or the teachers liked her. She had a ______________ for biting people and breaking toys, so finally the administrator told her mother to keep her home.

pensive **qualms** **patrician** **paucity** **quaff**

3. With her ______________ looks, the princess was perfect for the artist's series of royal portraits. He wanted to paint her staring off into the distance because it made her look ______________.

4. At the party, Serena would secretly ______________ soda from the bottle on the table. She had no ______________ about disobeying her mother, who had told Serena she could have only one glass. It wasn't because there was a ______________ of soda at the party; Serena's mother just didn't want her to have too much sugar.

query **personification** **rancid** **rabid** **penury**

5. The homeless woman lived in ______________; she wandered the streets and ate ______________ food from trash cans. She was the ________________ of our society's failure to take care of the poor in our country.

6. He was a ______________ Giants fan who attended every game, cheered when they won, and shouted insults when they lost. So, when he was given the opportunity to ______________ the coach about the Giants' losing streak, he jumped at it.

Exercise II Roots, Prefixes, and Suffixes

Study the entries and answer the questions that follow.

The root *matr/mater* refers to "mother."
The root *micro* means "small."
The root *bio* means "life."
The root *meter* means "measure."
The prefix *auto–* refers to "self."

1. Define the *italicized* target word.
   She had the necessary *maternal* instinct.
   The Amazon tribe was a *matriarchal* society.

2. List as many words as you can think of that contain the root *meter*.

3. Since *cosmos* refers to "world," a *microcosm* must be a ______________, while something that is *microscopic* is ______________, and a *microbe* must be______________.

4. List words that contain the prefix *auto–* and give a literal definition for each.

Exercise III Usage Inferences

Choose the answer that best fits the situation.

1. You would likely find someone described as *rabid*
   A. in the bleachers at a ballpark.
   B. in the hospital as a patient.
   C. at a school for gifted children.
   D. working at a convenience store.

2. You would likely find a ______________ in the room of a *pedagogue*.
   A. speech
   B. book
   C. brush
   D. painting

3. You would most likely find a *queue*
   A. in the reference section of a library.
   B. watching an international chess match.
   C. at the box office of a theater.
   D. at an insurance agency.

Exercise IV Reading Comprehension

Read the selection and answer the questions.

It seems to me that it was far from right for the Professor of English Literature in Yale, the Professor of English Literature in Columbia, and Wilkie Collins to deliver opinions on Cooper's literature without having read some of it. It would have been much more decorous to keep silent and let persons talk who have read Cooper.

Cooper's art has some defects. In one place in *Deerslayer,* and in the restricted space of two-thirds of a page, Cooper has scored 114 offenses against literary art out of a possible 115. It breaks the record.

There are nineteen rules governing literary art in the domain of romantic fiction—some say twenty-two. In *Deerslayer,* Cooper violated eighteen of them. These eighteen require:

1. that a tale shall accomplish something and arrive somewhere. But the *Deerslayer* tale accomplishes nothing and arrives in the air.
2. they require that the episodes of a tale shall be necessary parts of the tale, and shall help to develop it. But as the *Deerslayer* tale is not a tale, and accomplishes nothing and arrives nowhere, the episodes have no rightful place in the work, since there was nothing for them to develop.

3. they require that the personages in a tale shall be alive, except in the case of corpses, and that always the reader shall be able to tell the corpses from the others. But this detail has often been overlooked in the *Deerslayer* tale.
4. they require that the personages in a tale, both dead and alive, shall exhibit a sufficient excuse for being there. But this detail also has been overlooked in the *Deerslayer* tale.
5. they require that when the personages of a tale deal in conversation, the talk shall sound like human talk, and be talk such as human beings would be likely to talk in the given circumstances, and have a discoverable meaning, also a discoverable purpose, and a show of relevancy, and remain in the neighborhood of the subject in hand, and be interesting to the reader, and help out the tale, and stop when the people cannot think of anything more to say. But this requirement has been ignored from the beginning of the *Deerslayer* tale to the end of it.

Mark Twain

1. Which is not a criticism Twain expresses about Cooper?
   A. Cooper uses intellectual words that most people don't understand.
   B. Cooper's dialogues do not represent the way people actually speak.
   C. Most people who like Cooper's writing have not read much of it.
   D. The way Cooper writes his books is contrary to the rules of writing.

2. This selection is a good example of
   A. farce.
   B. satire.
   C. tragedy.
   D. drama.

3. The tone of this essay is one of
   A. somber reflection.
   B. humorous attack.
   C. bitter denunciation.
   D. sad regret.

4. The author states or implies that
   A. the literary critics he mentioned never read Cooper closely.
   B. Cooper was a writer who was underrated.
   C. Cooper was a master craftsman, but not much of a thinker.
   D. Cooper had a gift for portraying real people.

Lesson Eighteen

1. **accelerate** (ak sel´ ə rāt) *verb* to speed up over time
Recently, there was an automobile recall of millions of cars because they would unexpectedly *accelerate.*
ant: decelerate

2. **anaerobic** (an ə rōb´ ik) *adj.* existing without air or oxygen
Many odd organisms exist in the deepest parts of the ocean, where conditions are almost *anaerobic.*
ant: aerobic

3. **buoyant** (boi´ ənt) *adj.* able to float on water; cheerful or invigorating
If a steel boat is made large enough, it can be as *buoyant* as a wooden one.

4. **calibrate** (ka´ lə brāt) *verb* to check, fix, or adjust, based on a standard measurement
Scientists *calibrated* the total output of the new power plant after a year, and it surpassed their best expectations.

5. **commensal** (kə men´ səl) *adj.* in ecology, related to an animal or plant living with, on, or in another, without any injury to either
A huge number of *commensal* orchids twisted up the trunk of the tree, helping to shade it and using its bark as places for their roots.

6. **decompose** (dē käm pōz´) *verb* to rot or disintegrate; to return to simpler compounds
After only a few days' exposure to the open air, the dead fish had *decomposed* so much that it was barely recognizable.
syn: decay

7. **germicidal** (jer mi sī´ dəl) *adj.* having the ability to kill germs or other microorganisms
Besides being used as a cleaning agent, bleach also has tremendous *germicidal* qualities.
syn: antiseptic

8. **hematology** (hē mə täl´ ə jē) *noun* the study of blood and blood diseases
A good knowledge of organic chemistry and biology is necessary before even attempting to study *hematology.*

9. **host** (hōst) *noun* a plant or animal from which another obtains food or protection
Many types of clownfish use a sea anemone as a *host.*

10. **hypodermic** (hī pō derm´ ik) *adj.* applied under the skin, usually through a needle
The *hypodermic* needle needed to be at least two inches long in order to get the medicine deep inside the patient's muscle.

11. **immunity** (i mū´ ni tē) *noun* the resistance an organism has to infection or disease
Science has never been able to develop a vaccine that will provide *immunity* against the common cold.

12. **molecule** (mäl´ i kūəl) *noun* the smallest part of a chemical substance or compound made up of at least two atoms
It takes three atoms to make up one *molecule* of water—two atoms of hydrogen and one of oxygen.

13. **mutate** (mū´ tāt) *verb* to change or undergo transformation
During the experiment, cells began to *mutate* after being exposed to radiation.

14. **parasite** (pa´ rə sīt) *noun* an organism that lives in or on another life form and benefit while the other is harmed
Leeches used to be considered *parasites*, but they can also be helpful in treating some skin and blood diseases.

15. **symbiotic** (sim bē ät´ ik) *adj.* in ecology, related to an animal or plant living with, on, or in another, with benefits for both
Certain types of crocodiles have a *symbiotic* relationship with small birds that peck out particles from between the reptiles' teeth; the birds get food, and the crocodiles' teeth stay healthy.

Exercise I Words in Context

Fill in the blanks with the correct vocabulary words needed to complete the sentences.

accelerate **molecules** **calibration**

A. When a rocket is launched from Earth into orbit, it must ________________ to slightly over 25,000 miles an hour; otherwise, it cannot escape the effects of gravity. It takes about twenty minutes and thousands of tons of fuel to reach that speed. Scientific ________________ provides an estimate that if the rocket were powered by a few ________________ of material from a star, it would reach that speed within a second.

hematology **parasite** **host** **hypodermic** **mutate**

B. The unconscious patient was wheeled into the ________________ department of the hospital. Some type of ________________ had infected his body, and he needed an injection of strong antibiotics to combat the disease that ran through his circulatory system, which was acting as a ________________ for the destructive germs. The nurse prepared a ________________ needle and injected it into the man's arm. Everyone was confident that he would recover quickly, but, in a few minutes, the germs began to ________________ rapidly. Fortunately, the emergency doctors arrived with a different vaccine, and the patient survived.

germicidal **decompose** **immunity** **buoyant** **commensal**

C. The comedian started his routine by saying, "Nobody has ever invented a(n) ______________ against death. When I die, I want the funeral director to place my body on my mom's property to ______________ in the air. I want to establish a(n) ______________ relationship with her vegetable garden; I'll feed it, and it'll feed her. Every time it rains, I'll become ______________ and float to a different part of the garden to get a new view. I know she won't put any artificial chemicals or ______________ products on me, so I'll be a completely natural corpse."

anaerobic **symbiotic**

D. In the sand at the bottom of my fish tank, bacteria and microbes live in almost a completely ______________ environment, along with thousands of tiny worms. The microscopic creatures live off the waste that the worms produce, and the worms help keep the population of microbes steady. This odd ______________ relationship with each other helps keep the sand clean, which is the most important part of a healthy environment for my three large fish.

Exercise II Roots, Prefixes, and Suffixes

Study the entries and answer the questions that follow.

The root *aer* means "air."
The prefix *com–* means "together."
The prefix *para–* means "beside, near," "against."
The suffix *–ic/ics* means "relating to or characterized by."

1. Without using a dictionary, try to define the following words:

compress
compile
aerobic
aerospace
parallel
paranormal

2. Someone whose job is to travel to aid people who are ill or injured is called a ______________.

3. List as many words as you can think of that use the suffix *–ic/ics*.

Exercise III Usage Inferences

Choose the answer that best suits the situation.

1. Which sentence would be most likely be used to describe something *mutating*?
   A. For Halloween, I wore a pirate's costume.
   B. The caterpillar came out of its cocoon as a butterfly.
   C. That car is the most beautiful model I've ever seen.
   D. The world's oceans are becoming saltier each year.

2. Which would be the best example of *immunity*?
   A. Two people are put on trial for spying.
   B. A doctor develops a new type of heart surgery.
   C. Customers can't purchase advertised items.
   D. People get vaccinated against the flu.

3. Which of the following situations could be considered an example of a *symbiotic* relationship?
   A. I teach you to drive, I have a heart attack a year later, and you drive me to the hospital.
   B. You bake a birthday cake for my child, I invite you to the party, and she thanks you for the cake.
   C. I fix the roof on your house incorrectly, rain falls and ruins the carpet, and you sue me in court.
   D. You and I take the same math course, we study together, but I'm the one who fails.

Exercise IV Reading Comprehension

Read the selection and answer the questions.

Pythagoras the philosopher taught his followers to pray with a loud voice, but loud prayers do not appear to have been customary. On the contrary, it happened not unfrequently that the prayers were written on tablets, sealed and deposited beside the image of the god, so that no human being might be aware of the request contained in them. Besides sacrifice and prayer there is still another class of ceremonies in which we recognize the deep piety of the Greeks: first, the custom of *consulting* oracles, especially that of Apollo at Delphi, in times of great perplexity; and secondly, the universal practice, in cases of less or more sudden emergency, of trying to interpret the will of the gods by means of augury or *divination* in a vast variety of ways. Sometimes the augury was taken from the direction in which birds were observed to fly overhead. If to the right of the augur, who stood with his face to the north, good luck would attend the enterprise in question; to the left, the reverse. At other times an animal was slain, and its entrails carefully examined, the propitiousness of the gods being supposed to depend on the healthy and normal condition of these parts. But the gods were also believed to communicate their will to men in dreams, by sending thunder and lightning, comets, meteors, eclipses, earthquakes, prodigies in nature, and the thousands of unexpected incidents that occur to men. As few persons were able to interpret the bearing of these signs and wonders, there was employment for a large class of people who made this their particular business.

Finally, we must not forget to mention as a proof of the widespread religious feeling of the Greeks the national festivals, or games as they are called, established and maintained in honor of certain gods. While these festivals were being celebrated it was necessary to suspend whatever war might be going on between separate states, and to permit visitors to pass unmolested even through hostile territory. These festivals were four in number: the Olympian, Pythian, Nemean, and Isthmiafi.

Alexander S. Murray

1. According to the passage, what did the custom of "consulting oracles" show about the ancient Greeks?
   A. superstitious beliefs about predictions
   B. honoring of the oracles
   C. devotion to the oracles
   D. disregard towards the oracles

2. What did birds have to do with the practice of augury?
   A. Their color predicted the future.
   B. Their flights predicted the future.
   C. Their songs predicted the future.
   D. Their numbers predicted the future.

3. As explained in the passage, why were so many people involved in the job of making sense of the gods' methods of communicating to the ancient Greeks?
   A. The four festivals made understanding the gods important.
   B. When to plant crops made it necessary to understand the gods.
   C. Natural occurrences could mean disaster if they were interpreted incorrectly.
   D. Interpreting the will of the gods was difficult for most people.

4. Which sentence below is false, based on information in the passage?
   A. The prayers were frequently written on tablets.
   B. The gods spoke to people through dreams.
   C. The festivals were stopped because of wars.
   D. People needed to understand the gods in emergencies.